Gandhi and the Nuclear Age

Arne Naess

GANDHI
AND THE
NUCLEAR AGE

B̶P *The Bedminster Press 1965*

Preface

Today, upon the threshold of the Nuclear Age, the teachings of Mohandas K. Gandhi on group conflict have a special significance for us. We can, it would seem, no longer rely upon violence, or threats of violence, to safeguard what we hold to be of supreme value. But the trust we have lost in armed force has not been replaced in any appreciable way by a trust in nonviolence. The reduction of armaments, even if complete and universal, would provide no real solution to our problems: because of the present and future high level of research and arms technique, devastating and perhaps totally destructive nuclear and biological warfare can be waged in next to no time even after disarmament. Neither armament nor disarmament, then, can contribute substantially to a solution of the urgent problems of peace and survival which loom before us. When we turn, as we certainly must, to more profound and potent measures for world peace, Gandhi's teaching, based as it is upon a trust in nonviolence rather than upon a distrust of violence, will assume a great importance for us.

As long as we continue to think that the term 'passive resistance' means unarmed obstructionism, or confuse passivism with active pacifism, the incentive to study Gandhi will be weak. But nonviolence, as Gandhi has taught us, can be part of an offensive strategy. We find offensive nonviolence, as a matter of fact, not only in the work of Gandhi, but also in that of Danilo Dolci, Martin Luther King, Jr., Vinoba Bhave, and many others. In activities like theirs we find a form of resistance and *construction* at once nonviolent and active. If, as seems likely, the only means we have for dealing with international, racial and other greatly destructive conflicts are violence in defense or nonviolence in offense, it is overwhelmingly apparent that substantial efforts must, in the future, be directed toward the study and application of nonviolence.

We must, of course, ask how far Gandhi's special methods apply to conflicts on the international scale; one may argue, not without good reason, that they are quite inapplicable, or applicable only in a very indirect way. But we shall see, I hope, that Gandhi's contemporary significance does not stand or fall with its reference to any special *technique*. For beneath his techniques we can find important principles governing conduct in group struggle. It is these principles, ultimately, that are of great importance for us, rather than the special use made of them in specific situations by outstanding individuals.

One might well ask whether it would not have been better for this study to have taken an example closer to us: a moralist or politician from our Western culture. Why go so far as India? My answer is simple enough. I have not had the good fortune to encounter any Western substitute for Gandhi as a source of inspiration in the study of *group* conflict. Gandhi cannot be replaced by Thomas Hobbes, Friedrich Nietzsche, Albert Schweitzer, nor, indeed, by any other Western thinker or politician, since no one else has worked out a practicable ethics of group conflict, either as a self-contained department of ethics or as a branch of some more comprehensive doctrine. Gandhi alone can serve as our example; therefore this book has to be about him.

I wish to thank the Norwegian Research Council for Science and the Humanities for supporting the studies upon which this book is mainly based. I would like also to thank many persons for their help and interest in revising the original text, especially Professor Christian Bay, Mr. John Huot and Mr. Gene Sharp, M.A.

Arne Naess

Preface to the English translation

Since this little book was written in its original form in Norwegian, many former believers in the practicability of solving racial conflicts in a nonviolent manner have begun to have their doubts. It is time, therefore, to retrace our steps and to examine once more the teaching and example of the great leader in nonviolence, M. K. Gandhi.

I am grateful to Alastair Hannay for his efforts to translate the book into readable English.

A.N.

CONTENTS

Preface v

PART ONE: *Gandhi's Experience*

Gandhi—merely a man 3
It works 7
Lenin and Gandhi 16
*The empirical basis of Gandhi's nonviolent
     extremism 21*

PART TWO: *The Content of
     Gandhi's Political Ethics*

One basic principle and six fundamental hypotheses 27
Selected passages from Gandhi's writings 35

Avoid violence, but not by avoiding the conflict 39
*Did Gandhi overestimate the effect of nonviolence? His
    constructive program* 42
The psychology of trust 48
Gandhi and militant atheism 51
From principle to program of action 57
Satyagraha. Forms of action 62

PART THREE: *Gandhi's Political Morality
Compared to the Political Moralities of
Luther, Hobbes, Nietzsche, and Tolstoy*

Luther and Gandhi 81
Hobbes and Gandhi 92
Nietzsche and Gandhi 98
Tolstoy and Gandhi 102

PART FOUR: *Gandhi and International
Conflicts of Today*

Gandhi after India's political freedom 109
*The political significance of Gandhi's life and
    teaching* 113
Can nonviolent defense replace military defense? 120
Five programs for building nonviolent power 122

Notes 131
Selected bibliography of books in English 143

Part One

GANDHI'S EXPERIENCE

COUNSEL: However honestly a man may strive in his search for truth, his notions of truth may be different from the notions of others. Who then is to determine the truth?

ACCUSED: The individual himself would determine that.

COUNSEL: Different individuals would have different views as to truth. Would that not lead to confusion?

ACCUSED: I do not think so.

COUNSEL: Honestly striving after truth differs in every case.

ACCUSED: That is why the nonviolence part was a necessary corollary. Without that there would be confusion and worse.

(Gandhi examined by the Hunter Committee)

The individual is the one supreme consideration.
(Gandhi, in *Young India,* 13 Nov. '24)

Gandhi—merely a man

We find two diametrically opposed views of Mohandas K. Gandhi's moral stature. One has it that, ethically speaking, he was nearly perfect. Albert Einstein said of him, for instance, that generations to come would scarcely believe that such a man actually walked upon this earth. Moreover, in the collection of essays that appeared in 1949 under the title *Gandhi Memorial Peace Number,* Gandhi, as a moral being, was accorded the highest of praise by a large number of eminent persons. However, we also have to ask ourselves what was, exactly, the nature of Gandhi's contribution, and what is, exactly, the basis for the tremendous esteem and adulation in which he is held. For with regard to his own moral achievement, we find a second opinion which is, perhaps, as near the truth as the first, an opinion which has it that Gandhi was often mistaken and that it would be wrong to take him unreservedly as a moral example for everyone else.

The best known representative of this latter and more modest view happens to be Gandhi himself. There are other people who firmly accept that he fell short of his own very high aims. One of the best collections of Gandhi's teachings, *The Mind of Mahatma Gandhi*, compiled by R. K. Prabhu and U. R. Rao, opens with two chapters in which Gandhi speaks of his own personal imperfection, his mistakes, their painful consequences, and of his unrequited desire for help.

Many of his political opponents have maintained, moreover, that it was difficult in actual cases to bring Gandhi to the realization that he had made a mistake when he was convinced he had not; but even those criticisms do not detract from the sincerity of Gandhi's own declarations of imperfection. He saw as clearly as we can how uninhibited idealizing came to play a fateful role for him. We can see it by distinguishing three separate phases in his relationships with his supporters. In the first phase the relationship can be expressed as the attitude: "We won't manage any better with him, but it would be unwise to shake him off"; the second phase: "Together with him we'll certainly manage"; and the third: "He'll certainly manage *for us*." In the second phase Gandhi achieved his best work; in the third his contribution greatly diminished. His successes in that last stage came increasingly to be attributed to his own high moral attainments. He was already a saint, a demi-god. It became all too easy for people to think, "Whatever he says or does can't possibly have much to do with what I can do. I have no great moral ambition, nor any special abilities; I can't reasonably be expected to follow his example." By thus becoming clothed in a mystique of remoteness and divinity, Gandhi's words lost the special appeal they had when his prestige had not yet reached its peak.

The case of Albert Schweitzer presents a parallel. We have in him a man of outstanding ability, the recipient of several doctorates, an eminent musician, missionary, theologian, healer, and so on; how *can* such a paragon inspire ordinary mortals to action? Excellence of this order seems more likely to induce amazement and reverence than friendly cooperation. It is quite different, of course, if the man next-door goes off to Africa to start up a small hospital: knowing Jones as we do, we feel there are no real obstacles to our following in his footsteps should we feel so inspired.

Gandhi was never able, moreover, to make it sufficiently clear to his supporters that a nonviolent army needs soldiers and not just a general. When the crowds pressed in on all sides to touch him, they did not come to listen to what he said, or to work with him, they came for comfort. And these occasions were among the few when Gandhi lost his patience and showed anger. With Gandhi, as with others, reverence for the man himself is a product of the literature that grows up around him, but this literature in fact contains little support for the reverential attitude. The essential picture we get of Gandhi agrees less with that of his famous admirers than with his own.[1]

To describe Gandhi as a moral genius, however, would not be altogether absurd if what we want to stress is his constructive imagination and uncommon ingenuity in finding and applying morally acceptable forms of political action. In this field Gandhi was an Edison. He made incredible discoveries in the field of ethics and politics, and showed how to apply those discoveries. This, rather than any high moral level of his own conduct, is the truly remarkable feature of his achievement. Personally, of course, he did continually exert himself to maintain a high moral standard, but many people do that without ever making any moral discovery, any contribution to moral thinking and practice.

Gandhi earned the title "Mahatma," great soul, primarily because of the *effect* of his work. To understand this, we must see the difference between an external and an internal criterion of moral quality. According to an external criterion, we would judge an act good according to its consequences. According to the internal criterion, on the other hand, it would be the strength of the will to do good, the inflexibility of one's good intentions, that would count. In practical life, where it is primarily what people do that matters, we tend to measure moral value in terms of achievement, not intention; and for Gandhi too it was what was accomplished that mattered. So when we judge him we must bear in mind

Gandhi's experience 6

that from the practical viewpoint, great moral achievement need not presuppose a corresponding degree of
personal morality.

It works

Gandhi and his influence can be studied from many
points of view. In this book we shall concentrate mainly
on his teaching, and in particular on his direct instruc-
tion for group conflict. The first question, then, must
be: what is most characteristic and highly developed
in Gandhi's teaching? Perhaps we are inclined to answer immediately that it was his conviction that the use
of violence against living, sensible beings is never morally warranted, that it always infringes valid moral
principles. Accordingly, Gandhi's doctrine might be
summed up in one commandment: "Thou shalt not use
violence." But this would be highly misleading. The essential and most important point in Gandhi's doctrine,
taken as a whole, is not a principle or a commandment, but the working hypothesis that the nonviolent
resolution of group conflict is a practicable goal—despite
our own, and our opponents', imperfections; that nonviolent means are, in the long run, more effective and

reliable than violent ones, and that they therefore should be trusted even if they seem, for the moment, unsatisfactory. He teaches that nonviolence is a *practical* method which we may, no, *must,* adopt immediately and without hesitation in social, political, national, and international conflicts. And Gandhi is here talking to all of us, not mainly to politicians whose power is dependent on the opinions of others.

Understood in this way, the essential and most original aspect of Gandhi's teaching is his descriptive and explanatory account of man and of man's ability to resolve his own conflicts. In the realm of principles and metaphysics, Gandhi shows no remarkable originality.

Any systematic morality must base itself upon a number of purely descriptive or causal assumptions, as well as upon intuitive, normative notions; indeed, it is often precisely the emphasis it puts on one or the other of these two factors that gives a moral view its distinctive stamp; generally the tendency is for systems to lean toward descriptive and causal characteristics rather than toward intuitive and normative ones. It is therefore not so remarkable that new working hypotheses and methods covering group action can have immense import morally and normatively. Let us see what this general fact about philosophic systems can tell us about Gandhi.

There is nothing very original in condemning violence; and in any case Gandhi's condemnation of physical violence is considerably less radical and more qualified than that of many other moralists. The doctrine that violence and coercion against one's fellow humans are indications of moral poverty is to be found in the teach-

Gandhi's experience 8

ings of prophets, philosophers and wise men as far back as historical records go. In fact, among the generally acknowledged moral leaders from the time of ancient China and India down to the present day, the principle of nonviolence has been the rule, and the condoning of violence, even in defense, the exception. In ancient India not only was vengeance condemned, but the commandment "Thou shalt not kill" even extended to all animal life. However, alongside this there were often to be found pessimistically and fatalistically colored theories of human frailty and of man's inability to adhere strictly to such commandments. Evil nature and ignorance have usually been considered to be so deeply ingrained in man that general use of nonviolence in ordinary political and social struggle is thought to be impracticable. Or else the principle of nonviolence has been associated with the doctrine that nonviolent methods, even if the individual could and did employ them, would be ineffective in any extensive social and political conflict. In our own culture, influential studies of mass psychology have similarly stressed the impulse to mass violence, even if conceding also that men are peaceful enough individually.[2] All of these theories that "it will not work" are clearly anti-Gandhian, for Gandhi's teaching, in its essence and originality, is the straightforward doctrine that it *will* work, and that it can be shown to work. The proof of this for him lay in his own "experiments."

It follows that the focus of our examination of Gandhi's thought must be centered on his view of man and man's possibilities, especially on his faith in the possibility of mass action without violence, and in the possibility of influencing every individual by the example of nonviolent conduct. That this is the correct approach should be clear if we first base our study on, among other things, an examination of the contributions Gandhi made at the time when he was forming his ideas, that is, on a study of his activities in South Africa.

If the *originality* of Gandhi's teaching lies in his account of what men are constitutionally capable of, what it is in man's power to accomplish, it would nevertheless be misleading to say that his teaching was mainly of a descriptive character; it was the duties of man that he stressed above all. To UNESCO's inquiry about individual *rights,* Gandhi replied characteristically that primarily man has no rights, only *duties.*

Gandhi maintained that the key to his faith in nonviolence lay in his practical experience with men. And since he believed in the truth only of what he was able to test, we are in a position to test his own power of judgment, by going over and examining as far as possible what his actual experience with men was.

Research on Gandhi has so far neglected to view his activity from this standpoint; and although we cannot attempt any very comprehensive survey here, what we can and will do is to describe briefly some of his "experiments."

When the Boer War broke out in 1899, Gandhi, though his "personal sympathies were all with the Boers," felt that if he was to demand rights as a British citizen, it was his duty, as such, to participate in the defense of the British Empire. He "collected together as many comrades as possible [and] got their services accepted as an ambulance corps."[3] This was done only after great difficulties, however, since the British apparently thought his countrymen unsuited to carrying weapons, unsuited even to carrying stretchers on the battlefield, and hence consigned them to transporting dead and wounded behind the lines. However, Gandhi's men showed unexpected courage and were eventually accorded the "honor" of working in the front line. A few years later, during the so-called Zulu "rebellion" of 1906, Gandhi himself organized an ambulance corps, and this led him into contact with certain Zulus who had been flogged by the British. He and his corps also took care of men who had been burnt when the British set fire to villages. Had he chosen to he could have written an account of his experiences which would have caused consternation and horror, and which would have increased the bitterness and hatred that already existed. But instead of inflaming feeling, Gandhi did all he could to improve relations between the British and the Zulus. Thus we see him at this early stage, a courageous and influential man, already looking for positive solutions to the difficult problems of conflict.

Another instance is worth mentioning. Indians in South Africa had become embittered because by a judgment of the Supreme Court in 1913 the State was henceforth to recognize Christian marriages only. Indian mothers were thus considered unmarried unless married as Christians. As a consequence, political demonstrations by the women, something quite exceptional at the time, broke out. Gandhi succeeded, however, in getting the women actively involved in a wider struggle by persuading them to undertake a long march to the mines: the miners were then persuaded to stop work and to join the protest. Indignation grew to a high pitch when the men's wives were thrown into jail with male criminals.

Gandhi then persuaded the miners that whatever they did, they must avoid the use of violence, and he urged them to recognize that they would best attain their ends without violence and without breaking moral principles. The miners, between two and six thousand of them, without their women and children, then marched resolutely into the Transvaal, forbearing the use of violence of any kind; and this despite not only the repressive measures taken by the police against them, but privation and hunger as well.

This march strengthened Gandhi's belief in the ability of the common man to grasp the meaning of non-violence. The marchers were wholly illiterate; far from belonging to any culturally "enlightened" section of the community, they were, on the contrary, neither peaceful nor meek men by disposition, but men who were oppressed and who, seething with anger, had joined together to oppose repression and the discrimination shown against them.

Another case is even more illuminating. When a violent railway strike broke out which caused the Government to declare martial law, Gandhi's own campaign had not been progressing very well. But suddenly the Government's own position was rendered perilous and Gandhi held a very good card in his hand. Ordinary political strategy would dictate that he play this card, take full advantage of the situation, and enlarge the immediate goals of his campaign. But all Gandhi did was to enunciate once again his aims, adding that he had said that his goal, as it was then, and as it had been, was to bring about the end of racial discrimination. The railway strike, as he knew, could not help to persuade the opposition of the justice of his goal; quite the contrary, if Gandhi's forces were now to make use of the difficult position of the Government to push through their demands, they should have done so without persuading their opponent of the justice of the Indians' cause.[4]

So he broke off his campaign until the strike had ended. In the long history of political strife, this event must surely have few parallels. The impression it made was profound. Gandhi's opponents saw that he and his followers literally meant what they said when they claimed, *"this* and only this is our aim in *this* struggle." By not exploiting their advantageous position, Gandhi's supporters remained true to his and their own aim, which was future cooperation with those who were then their opponents. Gandhi was able to draw his own conclusions from the effect made by such a plea for moderation. If he had written a psychology of the masses, it would, no doubt, have been quite different from those which equate mass-man with the aggressive coward, for he had seen with his own eyes how the masses are capable of being led to two extremes, on the one hand to the most horrifying violence, and on the other to the most inspiring kind of nonviolence.[5] Gandhi knew, too, that through his action on behalf of the miners the mine owners were brought to the point of initiating reform; his action impelled them to a rational solution made in the spirit of compromise.

He had sought to base the agreement on the proposition that the opposed economic interests of employers and workers did not reflect any radical contrast of interests at a wider level. This point played a most important part in his work, and it is perhaps useful to compare here his activities with those of another revolutionary and friend of the workers who was campaigning at about the same time. The latter too exhorted men to strike; but an essential part of the strategy and tactics he employed involved violence and the power generated by hatred. This man made a sharp distinction between means and end. His name was Lenin. He practiced his beliefs, and history has shown the effect of his theories in Russia; but in South Africa and India, Gandhi practiced the precepts of quite another vision, the beneficial effects of which can be felt even today.

Another important introductory comment about Gandhi should be made here. As part of their struggle against communism, some Christian churchmen denounce Gandhi. They seem to see the figure of Gandhi standing in Christ's path and believe that only a Christian India can withstand the insidious advance of communism. However, quite apart from the dubious proposition that to undermine belief in Gandhi will be to the advantage of Christianity, the fundamental contrast between Gandhi and Marxist political morality is quite overlooked by such churchmen, for even today Christian theology and Marxist political morality seem far more compatible than Marxist and Gandhian morality. Gandhi's teaching, strikingly different from the moral principles of Marx and Lenin, appears to stand alone.

It might be objected, of course, that the combination of courage, sacrifice and devotion to humanity shown by Gandhi does not significantly distinguish him from many thousands, even millions, of forgotten men, who, in the course of history, have shown similar qualities. The greatest heroes of all time may have slipped by unknown and unacclaimed, or at least unrecorded. This may be true, but let us remember that Gandhi's "experiments" are not mentioned to illustrate any exceptional level of *morality*. Moral evaluations, at least those speaking of "courage" and so forth, assume an insight into another person's motives, and motives are things about which it is notoriously difficult to be conclusive. We should study Gandhi's "experiments with truth" only *within group conflicts* and quite apart from our convictions about their moral value. As I have already remarked, it is on the field of practical principle and action that our interest in Gandhi's teaching on conflict must mainly focus, not on the moral quality of his individual acts.[6]

Lenin and Gandhi

Some of Gandhi's fellow-workers, just as some of Nehru's in a later day, were Socialists and Marxists. Though critical of their views, Gandhi was far from negatively disposed toward their aims. He believed, however, that it could not be in the employers' interests to behave badly toward the workers, and that the employers could be induced to make radical reforms. On the basis of psychological and social interests common to both sides, he believed it impossible, in the long run, for one group to profit at the expense of the other. Exploitation and oppression amounted to violence, in

Gandhi's experience 16

Gandhi's terms, and could only drive participating elements in opposite directions.

Today we might well admit that the acceptance of Gandhi's view could have spared us Lenin's uncritical acceptance of means and also the kind of laissez-faire liberalism we find in Western Europe, a liberalism which rejects all measures of economic control to remedy the undeserved suffering of the poor. We have seen in our time how both of the political philosophies from which these economic views are derived have led to violence and oppression.

In John Ruskin, however, a liberal of a unique sort, Gandhi found a fellow critic of the economic establishment. In *Unto This Last* Ruskin speaks out forcefully against the dominant political economy of his day, a system which assumed hard and fast laws of supply and demand and an irresoluble opposition between employer and worker, and in particular an insoluble wage conflict ("the iron law of wages").

Ruskin had a sound knowledge of business and trade, and opposed the somber theories of his time by pointing to their practical consequences. He spoke out with great eloquence in the interests of mankind, claiming that the picture of man in current economic theory was but a caricature. As he said:

Observe, I neither impugn nor doubt the conclusion of the science if its terms are accepted. I am simply uninterested in them as I should be in those of a science of gymnastics which assumed that men had no skeletons. It might be shown, on that supposition, that it would be advantageous to roll the students up into pellets, flatten them into cakes, or stretch them into cables; and that when these results were effected, the re-insertion of the skeleton would be attended with various inconveniences to their constitution. The reasoning might be admirable, the conclusions true, and the science deficient only in applicability. Modern political economy stands on a precisely similar basis. Assuming, not that the human being has no skeleton, but that it is all skeleton, it founds an ossifiant theory of progress on this negation of a soul; and having shown the utmost that may be made of bones, and constructed a number of interesting geometrical figures with death's-head and humeri, successfully proves the inconvenience of the reappearance of a soul among these corpuscular structures. I do not deny the truth of this theory: I simply deny its applicability to the present phase of the world.[7]

Ruskin's argument, thus vividly expressed, suited Gandhi admirably, for it was just this idea, that economic life should be an autonomous sphere within the total common life of man, to which he was opposed, and which he found, in his South African experiences, his reasons to reject. There it had not been economic but ethical and political factors that had played the decisive role for the poor Indian minority; the conflict was not over prices or wages, neither for the Indians nor for their opponents. Thus it was not an insight into contemporary social economy that provided Gandhi with his basis for political reform, but an insight into human nature. Where many people saw only economic problems, Gandhi saw questions of the value of man, or, in our own non-Gandhian terminology, of "human rights."

After his return to India from South Africa, Gandhi carried out his first major campaign at Champaran in the province of Bihar. Property owners there had forced the peasants to cultivate indigo. Already poor, the peasants were put in an even worse plight when indigo began to be manufactured chemically. The plantations could scarcely compete with the manufacturers as the prices sank, and the employers were forced to cut their workers' wages. Driven to the edge of starvation, the workers became desperate, and violence erupted. If we now look at Gandhi's subsequent moves in Bihar, we will be able to see clearly the difference between a Gandhian and a Marxist treatment of conflict.

Gandhi's method showed, for a reformer, an extraordinary thoroughness in acquainting himself with the facts. He went directly to the district and organized systematic interviews for the collection of data. (Closely similar action, by the way, was taken by Danilo Dolci at the inception of his campaign in Western Sicily.) Thousands of workers were questioned. The resulting information went to make up a register compiling facts from all the factories and all the workers. In it were placed, among other things, extensive records of the many complaints that the workers had put forward. There was then a move for arbitration, as Gandhi had known there would be, and the factory owner came along with his witnesses; they too were subjected to the most detailed questioning. Naturally enough, the answers they gave supported the owner's point of view. But Gandhi was in a position to reply to them from the large fund of information he had gathered. He gave the workers, moreover, the confidence to stand up and repeat what they had told him in the interviews. The workers spoke out more and more freely in the presence of their employers and the representatives of justice. The information Gandhi had gathered was drawn on again and again in the discussions, and Gandhi himself acted as an intermediary in cooperation with both the officials and the plantation owners. When he argued against the owners, he first sent them a copy of his claims so that they could better defend themselves. And the legal authorities began, in their turn, to send copies of their documents to Gandhi.

Gandhi then brought the entire issue to a head by declining to accept any documents that he could not show to his fellow-workers. He insisted that a much greater confidence be placed in him, which it was; from then on the conflict took on quite a different character: each of the parties began to play with all its cards on the table.

Gandhi was not thus setting in motion a campaign based on a moral appeal to tolerance; he was initiating a serious process of data collection necessary to provide as detailed and many-sided a picture of the circumstances as possible. Moral conviction was not enough; the aim was to get his opponents to accept the information, and to see the facts of the situation without prejudice or self-righteousness. It was for this reason that Gandhi put himself and his information at the direct disposal of all his opponents.

In short, we can say that what Gandhi shared with Lenin was his understanding of the importance of a deep and careful study of economic and social factors before setting things in motion. Both were cool-headed men who lacked that occupational disease of many a moralist and revolutionary: an exaggerated trust in general statements and improvised action. Unlike Lenin, however, Gandhi always acted directly from his vision of man and man's possibilities, and never, therefore, took differences in economic interests or class conflict to be fundamental. Furthermore, he believed in a reciprocal interaction between ends and means, a belief which automatically excluded deceit and distrust as weapons in his struggle.

The empirical basis of Gandhi's nonviolent extremism

It was Gandhi's claim that the greater the efficiency he acquired in the use of nonviolence, the greater the impression nonviolence made on his opponents. This claim he held to be a legacy of his experiences in South Africa. Was he right in this? Did his claim follow, according to inductive principles, as a valid conclusion from what he saw?

The railway-strike episode and others of a similar kind did, in fact, provide Gandhi with an empirical basis for the hypothesis that the more he applied, even to fanatical extremes, the principle of nonviolence, the greater was its effect, and that every increase, no matter how slight, in the purity of the application of the principle meant an increase in the chances of success.[8] Thus we can see what was meant by Gandhi's seemingly extreme claim that if one man were able to achieve an entirely perfect, nonviolent method, all the opposition in the world would vanish. Yet we must be careful to note that Gandhi explicitly stated that we are all more or less imperfect, not least himself, and that therefore we can talk only in terms of degrees of success and not perfection.

Gandhi, then, had a satisfactory experimental basis for his claim that the consistent, or pure, forms of *satyagraha* (strictly, methods of holding on to truth) are more effective than the less consistent, or less pure, and that an increase in consistency, or purity, is especially favorable when a struggle is already well-advanced. He had, in other words, an argument for nonviolence over and above the purely moral one, and this argument is a strongly empirical and utilitarian one.

It may not seem so strange, then, that the versions which Gandhi's opponents gave of the political struggle agree with his own, for where nonviolence was at once most consistent and effective, no side suffered from the struggle itself or from its outcome.

When judging Gandhi's influence by the standards he himself set for empirical adequacy, we must subject it to the same rigorous critical scrutiny that we apply to any piece of scientific research. But we should note too the enormous complexity of Gandhi's experiments compared with ordinary experiments in, say, social psychology. The number of unknown, or insufficiently known quantities is overwhelming; so much so, in fact, that no conclusions can really claim the title of "scientific." Nevertheless, not all worthwhile research need culminate in well-founded scientific conclusions, nor need the unavoidable uncertainty of a conclusion cause us to reject it.

What, then, is our verdict to be? Judging from the material available to us, I think we may agree with Gandhi that his method in fact did work, and that the positive results of his action can to a large extent be traced to the nonviolence which characterized his campaign. Looked at as a *working hypothesis,* therefore, the conclusion that nonviolence can be a vital force in resolving conflicts appears to be a valid inference from the experiments in which Gandhi was involved, however few these "experiments" were.

Part Two

THE CONTENT OF
GANDHI'S POLITICAL ETHICS

One basic principle
and six fundamental hypotheses

Gandhi did not claim that the methods he used could be adopted as general models for all people and in all situations. He claimed they had no special significance or validity as methods independent of the personality and attitude of the man who employed them. By this Gandhi did not mean to imply that everyone who adopts them must share his religion and basic attitude; but he did mean that nonviolent methods can only be used in harmony with views of life characterized by certain common features. It would be beside the point to conjecture what philosophical views these would be; the best we can do is to study Gandhi's own position, especially in so far as it directly concerns group conflict. In what follows, therefore, we shall try to sketch a picture of Gandhi's political morality in terms of its principles and of its description of the world and man.

However, before proceeding, a possible misunderstanding must be reckoned with. We cannot assume, just because we can now construct a system based on our study of him, that Gandhi himself was systematic. It would be particularly wrong to assume that he arrived at his plans of action by applying a definite set of hypotheses and principles. This assumption would be especially unfortunate if it led us to judge Gandhi's actions solely in terms of his "system." For even if we were to reject one or more of the principles or hypotheses of that "system" we would still have to accept the fact that there was considerable value in the courses of action he initiated and himself undertook.

Confining ourselves to that part of Gandhi's teaching which directly concerns group conflict, we can find only one basic proposition of a normative kind. It can be expressed: "Seek complete self-realization."

Self-realization, briefly put, is the manifestation of one's potential to the greatest possible degree.

As Gandhi understood it, this principle can generate every other commandment or principle, that is, once we add to it certain hypotheses about man and the universe. The principle can be better understood, then, once we have stated the following three hypotheses:[1]

(1) Self-realization presupposes that one search for the truth.

(2) In the last analysis, all living beings are one.

(3) *Himsa* against oneself makes complete self-realization impossible.

Himsa may be translated as "violence," but it is better to retain the word *"himsa,"* since it signifies rather more than we ordinarily mean by "violence." Primarily, it is true, *himsa* does mean physical violence, or violence as we usually think of it, but it also covers coercion and duress in general, not all instances of which are necessarily physical. Resentment, for example, might be mentioned as a kind of *himsa;* for *himsa* covers not only inter-personal conduct, but also inner mental activity, that is, a person's feelings, attitudes and thoughts. In fact, the more we try to set limits to *himsa,* the clearer it becomes that what Gandhi was trying to express simply cannot be conveyed by any English word used in its normal sense.[2]

The opposite of *himsa* is *ahimsa,* and this expression, in Gandhi's time, was translated into English as "non-violence." We shall, in what follows, leave out the hyphen, reserving "non-violence" with a hyphen for a more general concept.[3]

The second hypothesis, that "in the last analysis" all living beings are one, can be expressed as the claim that all living beings are one *fundamentally;* this, of course, presupposes some standard for judging what is fundamental and what is not. And what is this standard?

Even the quite ordinary considerations of everyday

life make us each realize that it is impossible to consider ourselves simply as individuals occupying one narrow corner of space. We seem to extend beyond the very narrow confines of our hats and coats, however hard it may be to say exactly in what way and how far. If we ask ourselves what we want in this world, we inevitably discover that what we consider *our* own largely coincides with what other people consider *their* own. The happiness of other people is our happiness, their sorrow is ours; and so also with aims, ambitions, and the like. On the psychological and social plane, moreover, we find that an individual's development is continually dependent upon his capacity and willingness to identify himself with something more than himself, something with a greater individuality which yet comprehends his own. Usually we have no definite maximum in mind when we think of how far our relationships can go in this world, but for Gandhi there *was* such an ultimate basis of identification; he felt that the needs of his own self-expansion could only be satisfied by identifying himself with every living being. The "set" of which he saw himself a part was the total class of all living creatures.

Let us say by way of explanation that a progression can be traced, from an infant's inability to differentiate himself from the world he experiences, through the "solipsism" of his early childhood, to the affiliations of more or less mature citizenship in which he identifies himself in some degree with a particular country or form of government. He may even reach the elevated position of the cosmopolitan, the citizen of the world, in which, temporarily at least, he actually lives through the sorrows, doubts or pains of all who are in sorrow, uncertainty, or pain. By following Gandhi's train of thought, we should not only *discover* our own selves in their entirety, but should also thereby be able to *realize* our selves to the fullest possible extent.

Gandhi felt that man should know of both his place in the cosmos and of his own relation to other living things, and thereby discover, firstly, something he shares in common with all his kind, and secondly, the fact that the most important truths are precisely what is common to all life. Hence the *law of human life* is not at all "the law of the jungle." The laws of life and of the jungle were contrasted by Gandhi, and he believed that history would show a gradual abandonment of the latter, even in the affairs of governments and large groups, political, economic, social, and so on.

What validity can such a belief have? What can be the basis of Gandhi's interpretation, what the basis of an idea which Indian philosophers and philosophers of other countries supporting Gandhi, philosophers perhaps more original than he, have assented to? Any attempt we make to found the idea on an *argument* can only appeal to *intuition;* therefore an unequivocal appeal to intuition should be the one best source of verification. What we should say, moreover, that this appeal should be *to* is no doubt an experience of the kind we have in mind when we say: "When I was really concentrating, then I felt, though not in a way I can easily describe, that others and myself are one."

To confirm intuition, we often point to actual conduct which we take to be inspired by such intuition: a man acts toward another as if that man were himself, seeking what is best for him in the spirit in which he would seek it for himself. But clearly if we mean by confirmation some conclusive proof of intuition, or even some strong piece of evidence in support of it, then confirmation cannot be found; not surprisingly, therefore, it is difficult to find in Gandhi's writing any explicit foundation for this first hypothesis. In fact, he makes the search for truth a principle independent of his teachings on nonviolence. Nonetheless, implicit in his teaching on nonviolence is the conviction that it is only by a constant attempt to be truthful and objective in one's appraisal of the world around one that one can hope to realize the nonviolent principle.

The third hypothesis (see p. 29), that *himsa* against oneself makes complete self-realization impossible, assumes that by using violence we destroy something of ourselves, and hence preclude the possibility of developing our whole selves. The proposition that, in the last analysis, all living beings are one, presupposes a principle generated from these two hypotheses and the first principle, namely that one should avoid violence against any living being; otherwise complete self-realization would be impossible. The third hypothesis implies that "violence" in the widest sense against any living being at all makes complete realization impossible for the person who commits the violence.

Another important distinction has to be made: if I commit *himsa* against another, I necessarily work against my own realization, but not necessarily against his. If I hate somebody, it may be only myself that my hatred hurts.

Thus we have one principle and three hypotheses. Let us now add to these one more hypothesis which we derive from the first two. It is this:

(4) *Himsa* against a living being is *himsa* against one-self.

Then we may add a fifth hypothesis, derived from this last hypothesis and from the third hypothesis. It is this:

(5) *Himsa* against a living being makes complete self-realization impossible.

Finally, a sixth hypothesis, whose connection to the previous one is admittedly somewhat hard to determine:

(6) The kind of means used predetermines the end that can be attained.

As we shall see in what follows, Gandhi stresses that falsity can never lead to the victory of truth, nor violence lead to peace.

This presentation, despite the inclusion of some weak formulations, enables us to get an impression of the core of Gandhi's teaching on nonviolence. (As we noted before, it would be quite wrong to look on Gandhi as the originator of these teachings. They are to be found, for instance, in Indian philosophy long before the birth of Christ.) The most essential element of Gandhi's teaching on group conflict can be summed up in the following principle: Seek truth and realize *ahimsa*.

The term "pacifism" is used in many ways. Typically, however, it is the conscientious objector who comes to be labeled a "pacifist." The main belief of such a person, it seems, is that, on religious or moral grounds, he should not kill. However, his compunction about taking life does not necessarily include any equally strong maxim about engaging in nonviolent opposition to those who use violence. As a consequence some pacifists, simply wishing to have no part of violence, have withdrawn themselves from areas where violence reigns. Such withdrawal may, of course, require courage and may even result in great hardship. But the principle of conscientious objection *in itself* goes no further than the refusal to engage in violence. The Gandhian principles, however, do go further. There is therefore no reason to try to define the use of the terms "pacifism," and "Gandhianism" (or *"satyagraha,"* or "Gandhian nonviolence") in such a way as to make them synonymous. Quite distinct political moralities can emerge out of the different ways in which one takes the assertion *"Himsa* against any living being is *himsa* against oneself." According to the traditional pacifist principle of restraint from violence, the violence of other people is not damaging to one's own prospects of self-realization or to one's moral status. Consequently, the pacifist program leans toward withdrawal from, rather than engagement in, areas of conflict. However, by the principles Gandhi used in developing his program, it was consistent, indeed essential, actually to engage in conflict since one's self-realization was prejudiced as much by the violence of others as by one's own.

In the last few years, active anti-militarists and adherents of pacificist organizations have with increasing zest tried to develop the constructive elements of pacifist traditions. They have tried to convert defensive and passive anti-militarists into active participants in the conflicts of their age. This is certainly a development in accordance with the spirit of Gandhi.[4]

Selected passages
from Gandhi's writings

In the following pages are presented extracts from Gandhi's writings which should give the reader at least an indication of the written evidence relating to our account of Gandhi's moral teaching. Although the attempt has been made, as far as possible, to find statements which relate to the principle and hypotheses mentioned above, such statements are not selected because they specifically and exclusively support the interpretation so far given. The statements are representative of Gandhi's thoughts on the entire subject before us. Gandhi wrote:

1. If it is possible for the human tongue to give the fullest description of God, I have come to the conclusion that for myself, God is Truth. But two years ago I went a step further and said that Truth is God.[5]
2. "Nevertheless, your emphasis is always on *ahimsa*. You have made propagation of non-violence the mis-

sion of your life," argued the friend, still unwilling to concede the point. "There again you are wrong," answered Gandhiji. "*Ahimsa* is not the goal. Truth is the goal. But we have no means of realizing truth in human relationships except through the practise of *ahimsa*. A steadfast pursuit of *ahimsa* is inevitably bound to truth—not so violence. That is why I swear by *ahimsa*. Truth came naturally to me. *Ahimsa* I acquired after a struggle. But *ahimsa* being the means, we are naturally more concerned with it in our everyday life. It is *ahimsa,* therefore, that our masses have to be educated in. Education in truth follows from it as a natural end." [6]

3. I want to see God face to face. God, I *know,* is truth. For me the only certain means of knowing God is non-violence—*ahimsa*—love.[7]

4. If we had attained the full vision of Truth, we would no longer be mere seekers, but have become one with God, for Truth is God. But being only seekers, we prosecute our quest, and are conscious of our imperfection.[8]

5. . . . for me truth is the sovereign principle which includes numerous other principles. This truth is not only truthfulness in word, but truthfulness in thought also, and not only the relative truth of our conception, but the Absolute Truth, the Eternal Principle, that is God. There are innumerable definitions of God, because His manifestations are innumerable. They overwhelm me with wonder and awe and for a moment stun me. But I worship God as Truth only. I have not yet found him, but I am seeking after him.[9]

6. Literally speaking, *ahimsa* means "non-killing." But to me it has a world of meaning and takes me into the realms much higher, infinitely higher. It really means that you may not offend anybody; you may not harbour an uncharitable thought, even in connexion with one who may consider himself to be your enemy. To one who follows this doctrine there is no room for an enemy.[10]

7. I have been practising with scientific precision non-violence and its possibilities for an unbroken period of over fifty years. I have applied it in every walk of life, domestic, institutional, economic, and political. I know of no single case in which it has failed. Where it has seemed sometimes to have failed, I have ascribed it to my imperfections.[11]

8. In life it is impossible to eschew violence completely. The question arises, where is one to draw the line? Although essentially the principle is the same, yet everyone applies it in his or her own way. What is one man's food can be another's poison. Meat-eating is a sin for me. Yet, for another person, who has always lived on meat and never seen anything wrong in it, to give it up simply in order to copy me will be a sin. . . . Evil and good are relative terms. What is good under certain conditions can become an evil or a sin under a different set of conditions.[12]

9. Means and ends are convertible terms in my philosophy of life.[13]

10. I have often said that, if one takes care of the means, the end will take care of itself.[14]

11. They say "means are after all means." I would say

"means are after all everything." As the means so the ends. Indeed the Creator has given us control (and that, too, very limited) over means, none over the end. Realization of the goal is in exact proportion to that of the means. This is a proposition that admits of no exception.[15]

12. Though you have emphasized the necessity of a clear statement of the goal, but having once determined it, I have never attached importance to its repetition. The clearest possible definition of the goal and its appreciation would fail to take us there, if we do not know and utilize the means of achieving it. I have, therefore, concerned myself principally with the conservation of the means and their progressive use. I know if we can take care of them attainment of the goal is assured. I feel, too, that our progress towards the goal will be in exact proportion to the purity of our means.[16]

13. The way of peace is the way of truth. Truthfulness is even more important than peacefulness. Indeed, lying is the mother of violence. A truthful man cannot long remain violent. He will perceive in the course of his search that he has no need to be violent, and he will further discover that so long as there is the slightest trace of violence in him, he will fail to find the truth he is searching.[17]

Avoid violence,
but not by avoiding the conflict

Gandhi always gravitated toward the center of a conflict. Belonging as he did to a small group of wise men called *"karmayogi,"* his deeds accorded well with this designation, for *karmayogi* is the name for a yogi who seeks the highest end *through action*. A *karmayogi* does not isolate himself from a struggle; he remains at the very heart of it, immersed in the conflicts of his fellow men as one among them. From the center of the struggle he tries to bring about a *general* reduction of violence, instead of avoiding it himself. It is not enough to put oneself *hors*

Avoid violence 39

de combat; hence the principle, "Act in group struggle, and act, moreover, in a way conducive to the long-term, universal reduction of violence."

Two statements by Gandhi are particularly important here. First:

To see the universal and all-pervading Spirit of Truth face to face one must be able to love the meanest of creation as oneself. And a man who aspires after that cannot afford to keep out of any field of life. That is why my devotion to Truth has drawn me into the field of politics.[18]

and secondly:

I could not be leading a religious life unless I identified myself with the whole of mankind, and that I could not do unless I took part in politics. The whole gamut of man's activities today constitutes an indivisible whole. You cannot divide social, economic, political, and purely religious work into watertight compartments.[19]

By being compliant, and by living in modesty and seclusion, it is certainly possible to avoid committing violence, possible even to avoid *himsa* itself, in its more exacting senses. But what good is that if other people still go on using violence? In any case, to disengage ourselves from a conflict often means indirect support of the violence we put ourselves above, an indirect support suggesting that we are content to leave the fighting to those who are less particular about the means to be adopted, though the cause be one we would really like them to win for us. But Gandhi's principle states that *all himsa*—one's own or that of others—directly affects every one of us. It is thus diametrically opposed to a pacifism which preaches involvement in only a narrow personal responsibility for nonviolence.

Let us take an example. During the political struggles between the Imperial authorities and the freedom movement in India in the 30s, students organized the boycott of a university. They lay on stairways and pathways in order to hinder those who did not want to join in their action. Gandhi spoke out against this:

It is degrading to the opponent to step on people and because it is degrading he will not do it. But he will hardly be less embittered, and it has nothing to do with the affair in hand whether he has a high ethical standard and does not want to step on others, or whether he defies the action and fills the auditoriums.[20]

Such conduct, Gandhi observed, would not diminish the opponent's hatred, and why should it? Admittedly the opponent might be brought to the point of not entering the university, but the reasons he would have for not entering would not necessarily stem from the right source. Indeed, such action might easily result in making the struggle more bitter than before.

A famous passage from St. Matthew (v, 39-44) is an excellent illustration of the difference between nonviolence and passivity: "But I say unto you, That ye resist not evil: but whosoever shall smite thee on thy right cheek, turn to him the other also." This extract, together with the whole passage from which it comes, has received a number of different and mutually incompatible interpretations in theological literature. Sometimes, but not often, it has been taken to express an actively nonviolent standpoint. By others, however, it is interpreted as a recommendation of non-interference with the perpetrators of violence, non-participation at all costs, however great the provocation. But as we have seen, there can, according to Gandhi, be a nonviolence that is on the offensive, an active participation in conflict that violates no requirement essential to moral virtue. Gandhi saw this as a principle moving him to pursue his positive aim *regardless* of the blows that would be directed at him from all quarters. Gandhi saw that he must remain true to this aim, an aim that he recognized as one common to himself and all who opposed him.

Thus, one does not "turn the other cheek" in order to confuse or bewilder or *cast* shame on the aggressor: one *disregards* the aggression and simply does not *try to avoid* a blow on the other cheek. Active nonviolence concentrates on the positive goal, whatever the provocation.

Did Gandhi overestimate the effect of nonviolence? His constructive program

When making optimistic forecasts about the outcome of the struggle for freedom in India, Gandhi used to say that success depended on increasing the constructive programs. But since these always fell short of what Gandhi required, his forecasts were not wrong, but simply rendered invulnerable to criticism. If the main effort of the nationalist movement was expended on opposing the British, according to Gandhi, nothing good would come of it. But his advice to concentrate upon constructive planning, rather than upon fighting the British, was not taken seriously by the politicians who were ostensibly his adherents. Naturally, such advice had little appeal; it demanded discipline and self-sacrifice.

Perhaps Gandhi failed to repeat his great warning often enough. We should at least remind ourselves of this possibility when judging his sensational prediction in 1920 that India could free herself from Britain within a year. Naturally enough, this statement earned him both criticism and ridicule.[21] But Gandhi himself wrote: "Much laughter has been indulged in at my expense for having told the Congress audience at Calcutta that if there was sufficient response to my programme, of non-cooperation, swaraj [freedom] would be attained in one year."[22] He had appealed to his countrymen to support his constructive efforts and called on them to form their own unofficial institutions and their own economy, in addition to their campaign to break away from British institutions and reliance on British imports. In other words, Gandhi could only envisage *swaraj* on the assumption that his positive demands were to be taken up and *acted upon*. But relatively few people did act upon them. "The conditions I had set for the fulfilment of the formula ['*swaraj* in a year'] were forgotten."[23]

Gandhi was no doubt perfectly correct in his view of

what was needed before *emancipation* from British power could become a reality: emancipation is, after all, certainly a loftier goal than political independence. But he must have overestimated the capacity of his followers and fellow campaigners to follow the principles he prescribed. And there is perhaps an explanation for this; Gandhi seems occasionally to have interpreted all *absence* of physical violence as the *presence* of nonviolent action. Moreover, constant repetition of "non-this" and "non-that," especially of "non-*violence*," must have tended generally to make it seem natural that the work of creating institutions and patterns of moral activity should be subordinated to a negative aim, the avoidance of violence. Nevertheless, an exact analysis of Gandhi's teachings seems incontrovertibly to show that it was the positive and constructive factors that were his first concern, from which the absence of physical violence was intended to emerge as a natural, and perhaps inevitable, *consequence*. It is a familiar enough fact, after all, that aggressive tendencies tend to disappear among those who are intensively occupied in constructive work.

Here, as at other points in Gandhi's career, we can readily deplore the effect, if such it was, of giving prominence to that one key word *ahimsa*. For to undertake a complicated reform movement requiring a program of construction, the concept of "nonviolence" appears not at all suggestive of that vast amount of energy and initiative which would have to be expended in the process.

Gandhi's great admirer, Romain Rolland, once asked how the Mahatma's voice sounded, for he was greatly interested in how Gandhi's words were able to reach one hundred million people. He received the reply, across the table, that Gandhi spoke "no louder than we are doing now." "But then, how can people hear him?" asked Rolland. "They don't hear him," was the answer.[24] Although crowds streamed to his meetings, only those people who got nearest to him could hear what he was saying. The rest heard nothing. And if they could not hear his teaching, neither could they read it, since most of them were illiterate. In fact, they could hardly have been expected to have any clear idea at all of his moral and political ideas. From the large correspondence Gandhi had with people who had personal access to him, it appears also to have been enormously difficult for people to grasp the meaning of Gandhi's teaching. Certainly it was by no means obvious to the Hindus, nor was it part of their living tradition, as is often maintained.

The most difficult parts of his teaching are those principles of the positive program. It was here that Gandhi entered into the daily life of the individual. What he demanded was a new way of living. Above all, the Indian had to learn to fend for himself. "To get swaraj . . . is to get rid of our helplessness," said Gandhi.[25] And if their helplessness was really to be conquered, it would be an advantage, for the time being, he said, to keep the British in the country.

How many of Gandhi's adherents and admirers stood beside him, actually understanding what he said on this topic, believing it was right, and trying to act upon it? Almost none. Among the politicians, practically no one accepted his teaching; neither Nehru nor any of the other prominent personalities who were daily praising Gan-

Constructive program   45

dhi.[26] Practical efforts of immediate and immense importance, such as the setting up of nonviolent brigades in all trouble-centers, were therefore never actually made, in spite of pressure exerted by Gandhi.

There was, after all, a vast difference between the practicability of Gandhi's work in South Africa and in India. In South Africa he was able to come into personal contact with all those he was fighting for, and also with his most important opponents. The political forces were there less complex, the aims simpler and the country smaller. So if one is looking for examples of campaigns of nonviolence in their purest form, and carried out with the clearest awareness of what was involved, one must look to the events in South Africa outlined earlier.

Gandhi did lay himself open to criticism for expecting, from time to time, immediate and far-reaching effects from nonviolent methods. He should surely have known that it is easier to get millions to join together in a single short-lived campaign than it is to change the daily habits even of a few men in the extensive way he required—a way involving community service, assistance for neighbors in need, patience in attempts to integrate asocial elements into society, and non-partisanship in the permanent friction between Hindus and Muslims, etc. Gandhi's methods required local leadership throughout India, and they required a large number of men who could devote themselves to the duties of community service in every aspect. Gandhi was indeed making enormous demands within the framework of the positive program. Moreover, as is evident from his constantly reiterated hopes for a turn to the better during the 1920s, he waited a long time before drawing any pessimistic conclusions. But the turn never came; and, as a result, the freedom India won was only a political freedom, not the complete *swaraj* which Gandhi fought for: not the inner and the outer emancipation and ripening, not the cessation of communal hatred.

To return for a moment to the metaphysical foundation of Gandhi's political morality, we can now present the principles of his positive program more lucidly, not only as part of but as central to his teaching as a whole. Consider once again the hypothesis, "In the last analysis all living beings are one," and the principle, "Seek complete self-realization." Let us replace the hypothesis, "Violence against a living being is violence against oneself" with the hypothesis, "Complete self-realization presupposes the self-realization of everyone."[27] The main point is that with this change we omit talk of violence. Instead, we have hypotheses and principles about positive influence and active help, reminiscent indeed of Pëtry Kropotkin's principles of mutual aid.[28]

Gandhi said that one must forget the self in one's constant and enduring service to all life. Gopinath Dhawan has shown how this statement can be interpreted: "The real being in man, the central truth in him, is the spirit. The spirit is one in all, and to realize this great truth 'one has to lose oneself in the continuous and continuing service of all life'."[29] Thus the doctrine of nonviolence can be subordinated to a doctrine of consistent altruism or, better, to one of mutual aid (in which "service" emerges as

Constructive program

a natural consequence, rather than standing merely as a rule of conduct), along with the hypothesis, "Violence helps no one to self-realization."

By altering the sequence of principles and hypotheses in this way, the principles for a positive program can be directly derived from a basic principle for group conflict, namely, "Act in all group conflicts, and act with a view to helping all parties in the conflict." Not the least important implication of this idea is that to acquire such a universal consciousness of conflict it is necessary to train oneself in all aspects of community service. Thus the separate aspects of Gandhi's positive program can be better understood.

These remarks show, among other things, how we may change the emphasis of a doctrine without changing its metaphysical foundations.

The psychology of trust

Many of Gandhi's actions were, on the face of it, demonstrations of sheer lunacy. For instance, in 1931 he went unguarded into the textile manufacturing areas of England, though told that he would certainly be killed if he did so. The terrible unemployment of that year had hit the textile workers especially hard. Indians were no longer buying textiles to the extent that they had done before. Moreover, the campaign for home industries which Gandhi had organized in India had had a powerful effect, and the British Press was not slow to blame Gandhi for the sufferings of the workers. In fact the newspapers, eager to find a scapegoat for the dreadful privation and suffering of their public, greatly exaggerated and distorted his role.

In spite of all warnings, Gandhi went to the workers, defenseless and trusting. And it was not just to show sympathy with the textile industry's view of the crisis that he went. On seeing the textile workers' actual living conditions, he pointed out to them how fantastically rich they were, compared with the poor of India, and he followed up this surprising statement by saying that the economic aims of the textile industry were unrealistic; they had not been formulated, he said, with any understanding of the European crisis as a whole. One would expect such words to have provoked bitter reaction, but Gandhi's manner, marked by humor, trust, respect, and compassion, made it extremely difficult to oppose him. The workers gave him time to present his views, and they managed ultimately to divert their hatred from individual persons. They ceased to be his enemies and became his potential fellow-workers.

Trust in others, moreover, played a unique role under the (to Western eyes) strange conditions prevailing in the places in which Gandhi's closest disciples lived.[30] Trust was extended even to scorpions and snakes. Gandhi's faithful fellow-worker, Miss Madeleine Slade, says that even with these creatures creeping about in the *ash-ram,* no serious accident took place. Gandhi held a theory that not only men, and children, but even animals more or less intuitively perceive an attitude of trust. Indeed, a sign of defensiveness or uncertainty may be seen, or felt, as we know, by an animal long before it is detected by a trained psychologist; he who can harbor feelings of fear is always a potential enemy.

This theory about trust is part of the psychological background of much of what Gandhi meant; and he meant it as *realpolitik* rather than as utopian idealism. Yet few people have followed his injunction to awaken trust in place of fear, and the reason for this is surely fear itself. Fear is deep-seated; it possesses us, and it is mainly the force of fear itself that prevents its removal. Fear cannot be fought, it has to be replaced. If you force yourself to convey an impression of unconcern and fearlessness, you will most likely fail; others will be able to see your pretence and your fear. Where fear can be removed (and one of the places where it can is in personal relationships), it can only be removed, as Gandhi said, by putting trust in its place.

Thus personal contact was not only a significant element in the nonviolent campaign; it was, for him, a decisive one. His belief in its importance grew from personal experience, experience which showed him that in another person, literally whoever he is, there is always something one can appeal to with confidence. And even if one's opponent acknowledges the appeal only reluctantly, and with every qualification he can summon, he will not succeed forever in preserving the appearance, or the fact, of his indifference or implacability. If a man can be approached, there is a chance, possibly only one chance, that he will relent. However, he must be convinced of the sincerity of the approach. Gandhi wrote, "I hold it an axiomatic truth that real *ahimsa* never fails to make an impression on the opponent." [31]

Gandhi and militant atheism

Gandhi's attitude toward atheists and atheism has seemed to many people both paradoxical and inconsistent. What are we to say of his oft-repeated assertion that atheism could be part of the truth, so long as the atheist was as committed to his atheism as the theist to his theism? This from a man who not only regarded himself as an orthodox Hindu but also professed Godlessness to be nothing less than an abomination? It is of vital importance to be clear on this matter, since Gandhi's attitude toward atheism can provide a key to our understanding of his position on theoretical issues in general.

We can gain a sense of this position partly in his transition from one to the other of the affirmations, "God is Truth" and "Truth is God," partly in his attitude to other religions, and partly in the great weight he put on individual religiosity. His own statements indicate just how embracing his view of religion was, and these views enable us also to understand how it was that he could work together with atheists; for he conceived the aggressive morality of atheism as a genuinely religious attitude. Gandhi wrote:

As a tree has a single trunk, but many branches and leaves, so there is one true and perfect Religion, but it becomes many, as it passes through the human medium. The one Religion is beyond all speech. Imperfect men put it into such language as they command, and their words are interpreted by other men equally imperfect.[32]

This passage goes far to explain as well as demonstrate Gandhi's tolerance for other religions.

An atheistic social worker, G. Ramachandra Rao ("Gora") has written a little book, *An Atheist with Gandhi*, which tells of his attempt to secure Gandhi's active help and support for humanitarian work based on atheistic principles. Apparently Rao specialized in arranging cheap "cosmopolitan" dinners to which people of all castes and religions were invited. To these gatherings he also invited the caste-less, thus breaking with all custom and convention. Rao's idea was that the assembled company should feel as one family. The same intention to foster brotherhood in place of identification with specific caste and religion informed his encouragement of marriages between caste and non-caste people. Atheism, so Rao thought, could be of the greatest help in dissolving those forces that divided society against itself. But he not only believed atheism to be an effective and constructive tool, he preached this belief and urged men first to accept all human ends as earthly, and secondly to reject such theories as the transmigration of souls and fatalism.

What was Gandhi's reaction, then, when Rao appealed to him for advice on how best to accomplish his work? At first Gandhi was negative. He wrote in 1941: "Dear Friend, Atheism is a denial of self. No one has succeeded in its propagation. Such success as you have attained is due to your sincere work among the people round you. I am sorry I cannot invite you to come here. I have no time to spare for talks." [33]

Three years later, however, one of Rao's fellow workers had a chance to meet Gandhi at Sevagram Ashram. Pyarelal, Gandhi's faithful secretary, has recorded a conversation about atheism between the two men. On being asked about the relationship between God and man, Gandhi began his reply by saying, "I used to say 'God is Truth.' That did not completely satisfy me. So I said 'Truth is God.' He and His law are not different. God's law is God Himself. To interpret it man has to resort to intense prayer and merge himself in God." Gandhi went on, "You may call yourself an atheist, but so long as you feel akin with mankind you accept God in practice." [34]

Rao reports how his own first meeting with Gandhi opened with characteristic good humor. He says, "He greeted me with a broad smile and the first question: 'What shall I talk to a godless man?' We both laughed heartily and I replied, 'Bapuji, I am not a godless man, I am an atheist.' " [35]

Gandhi and militant atheism 53

The distinction between godlessness and atheism was one that Gandhi accepted completely. His teaching was directed against godlessness, and only indirectly aimed at atheism. That he did, even indirectly, attack atheism was due to what he considered its false assumptions and evil consequences. Gandhi thought that even if there were individual atheists who were not godless, the doctrine of atheism was likely to help the spread of godlessness.

In Rao's view, atheism allowed those who have resigned themselves to fatalism or to the divine will to regenerate themselves to believe once more in themselves, in their power to decide and act, and in the possibility of social reforms. Gandhi, however, appears to have been unconvinced about these effects and said that he might fast against the spread of atheism, to which Rao immediately replied, "I will fast against your fast." [36] This seems to have convinced Gandhi that Rao's atheism was a deep, personal conviction. The ice, in any case, had been broken; Gandhi asked Rao to stay in his *ashram,* and later, in fact by 1945, Rao had become almost a regular member. Neither he nor his atheistic friends attended the daily prayer meetings and "none seemed to mind my absence." [37] In addition to manual labor, Rao was entrusted with the teaching of science to the nurses of the Ashram Hospital.[38]

When Rao, himself a Brahmin, was going to give his daughter in marriage to an "untouchable" (a caste-less man), Gandhi agreed to act in the ceremony, in which the words "in the name of Truth" were to be substituted for "in the name of God." And why should the change not be made? "Do you think I am superstitious?" asked

Gandhi. "I am a superatheist. . . . The concepts of truth may differ. But all admit and respect truth. That truth I call God." [39] The wedding ceremony was to take place in April, 1948, but Gandhi died in January. That March an atheistic marriage ceremony was performed by deputies for Gandhi. Naturally enough, Rao felt Gandhi was the atheists' friend and protector; he says: "The assassination of Gandhiji meant a terrible loss to civilization; it is as much a loss to atheism." [40]

How was Gandhi able, as an orthodox Hindu, to extend himself so far toward atheism? The question is badly put; Gandhi distinguished between atheists and atheism. The latter interested him very little in his dealings with Rao. Generally it appears he was unwilling to get involved in such theoretical distinctions. The interesting thing to Gandhi was: What is Rao doing? What leads him to act thus? In exactly the same way, the significance of his own actions lay in the answers he himself gave to these questions; theoretical discussion could not provide the answer. Adopting what might seem to us an unequivocally pragmatic criterion of truth, Gandhi found his answers in the actions of men. In order to judge Rao's position, he had to become acquainted with Rao, his family, and his work. The impression these gave him provided Gandhi with a positive answer. He writes in a letter: "Though there is a resemblance between your thought and practice and mine superficially, I must own that yours is far superior to mine." [41] In this light we can understand more easily his attitude toward atheism, that is toward Rao and other personally convinced, militant atheists.

Gandhi and militant atheism   55

In his book Rao puts great stress on Gandhi as a humanitarian reformer, and thinks he would have gone over to atheism had he thought atheism could end men's suffering.[42] Now Gandhi felt that he and Rao were both seeking the truth, though neither had found it. And surely it is this which explains Gandhi's attitude to him; this together with his belief that morally satisfactory results in an "experiment with truth" are a sufficient indication that one is moving in the right direction, and that it is only the direction, not the goal, that one can know with certainty. To Rao, he says, in a concluding remark, "I see an ideal in your talk. I can neither say my theism is right nor your atheism wrong. We are seekers after truth. We change whenever we find ourselves in the wrong. I changed like that many times in my life. . . .Whether you are in the right or I am in the right, results will prove. Then I may go your way or you may come my way; or both of us may go a third way. So go ahead with your work. I will help you, though your method is against mine." [43]

The high value Gandhi placed on the individual's will to seek what is true, and his recognition of every man's duty to help another to follow his chosen path even when he feels that that path might lead nowhere, or perhaps even to danger for us all, inevitably invites misunderstanding. If we ask what Gandhi's position is on this or that question, or what actions and political programs he supports, we will get no one answer. The questions have to be rephrased. We have to ask not only what Gandhi's position is with respect to this or that, but what is his attitude to this or that adherent of this or that. Abstracted from those specific procedures, those particular attributes which characterize it, a program of action was for him little more than a mode of belief, something that might only, if strong and popular, affect people in this way or that. As the creed of a dedicated man, however, a program of action was to be judged principally by that man's will and capacity to seek out the truth.

In this light we may more readily understand why Gandhi's theism stood not at all in the way of supporting an atheist, or of recognizing the possibility that an atheist might come nearer to the truth than Gandhi himself.

From principle to program of action

How did Gandhi set about realizing his principle: "The essence of non-violent technique is that it seeks to liquidate antagonisms but not the antagonists"? [44]

It has long been the custom to speak of nonviolent as contrasted to military *methods and techniques*. But it should be noted that the distinguishing feature of a method or technique, as such, is that it is a mere instrument; the goal or aim toward which it works is something else. It is not necessary that the method or technique should have more than an instrumental value;

only that it be employed unflinchingly toward the end in question. The kind of conduct Gandhi employed in group-conflict can, to some extent, be made into an organized system, but only to some extent; if the aspect of *method* is overstressed, we find ourselves interpreting Gandhi's teaching as a kind of cook-book doctrine. One forgets his maxim: "Means and ends are convertible terms in my philosophy of life."

In any campaign, according to Gandhi, moral principles *must* be observed. Such principles concern a man's purity of intention, his respect for other individuals, and the absence in him of any tendency to look upon his fellow beings as means to an end. During campaigns, therefore, virtuous actions are to be performed, in part, because it is one's duty to perform them, not merely because of advantages one hopes to reap from performing them.

Looked at from the outside, *satyagraha* seems to be a set of *methods;* it appears to be a means to an end. And this is because it is characteristic of a bystander, as opposed to a participant, to concentrate on the efficacy of nonviolence in a conflict, and to consider the importance of integrity or purity of intention for attaining an end. Integrity, however, just cannot be objectified or even described as a technique.

It is possible, of course, during a campaign to switch from the observer's position to the participant's and back again. It is possible, that is, for someone to *use* nonviolent *means.* But if in using them, the element of *means* is what consistently motivates one's conduct, then as a participant one loses one's integrity—one's purity of intention, in the terminology of Gandhi—and one's campaign is essentially futile even if victorious in some superficial way.

At the moment when a bomb is released it clearly makes not one whit of difference what the attitude of the man who released it was. The bomb triggers a long chain of events on its own. Since it was Gandhi's purpose not only to dispense altogether with weapons, but to put something in their place, it is only to be expected that people should look upon nonviolent standards of behavior and performance very much as they look upon weapons—as means whose effect is largely independent of the attitude of those who adopt them.

It is not difficult, however, to avoid the dangers of this analogy with weapons. It is enough to say that the principles of a nonviolent morality must remain in force at the time when nonviolent methods are being "used." These principles themselves prescribe a standard of behavior, and a standard of behavior cannot in practice be reduced to the "use" of a "method."

The attempt to limit and reduce the use of weapons has today, quite reasonably, a high priority, in the minds of national leaders, but in the long run it seems clear that each of us must consider another and even more central problem, the problem of whether man is to survive *as a man;* the problem, that is, of finding and implementing principles of group struggle which do not violate fundamental moral requirements.

We can, generally speaking, divide Gandhi's activity

From principle to program   59

with respect to group conflict, prior to his adoption of *satyagraha* (in its specific Gandhian form), into five stages, which are:

(1) The non-partisan analysis of a conflict and of its background;
(2) The clarification of essential and long-range interests which the conflicting groups have in common;
(3) The definition of reasonable, long-range aims which all of the contending parties might envisage and agree to;
(4) The formulation of such aims in a precise and concrete way, and an attempt to ensure that the contending parties understand them (Gandhi emphasized the importance of so describing an end as not to leave even a shadow of doubt that it is completely warranted and understood.);
(5) In the case of the persistent refusal by one party to accept the aims as so defined, an attempt at compromise by making unessential changes in the definition.

If all this failed, Gandhi then considered himself justified in setting *satyagraha* in motion. Once he had adopted *satyagraha,* he carried it through to the end, cost what it may, even life itself.

In order to ensure the invariable success of *satyagraha,* it must be assumed:

(1) that there can always be found some interest common to all of the contending parties;

(2) that the parties are, or might be, amenable to an "appeal to heart and mind";

(3) that those who are in a position to start applying *satyagraha* are also in a position to carry it through to the end.

On the strength of his considerable experience, Gandhi was certainly justified in accepting these three assumptions as *a basis for action*. (Naturally, the matter will appear quite otherwise to those of us who have had no such experiences or who are considering matters only theoretically.)

We are able, upon reviewing Gandhi's thought, to distinguish between what is essentially *realpolitik* and what is essentially an ethical argumentation posed by the man. The significance of the former, and the faith he had in it, rests in what he took to be the limited power of moral appeal. Rabindranath Tagore wrote in one of his critical letters in 1922, referring to acts of violence committed by the masses led by Gandhi: "It is difficult to avoid violence for long when the mind is continually inoculated with thoughts that stimulate hate. A complete non-violence (Ahimsa) can only exist when hostile thoughts are rooted out. That is the truth. It cannot be attained with simple moral injunctions, even when they come from a person such as Gandhi." [45]

According to Gandhi, to give an accurate account of a conflict, to get clear about common ends with one's antagonist, and to have faith in one's ability to induce his cooperation were essential steps toward rooting out hostile thoughts. The mind, when it is not continu-

From principle to program 61

ally "inoculated with thoughts that stimulate hate," can develop a broad view of life, can develop tolerance and sympathy with an opponent's situation, and thus an understanding of the struggle and problems he also faces.

The difficulties of conducting a campaign in accordance with Gandhi's principles are obviously present in each of the phases of the campaign which precede *satyagraha*. If those phases are not correctly understood, there can be *no* adequate *satyagraha*. Those five preliminary stages make quite unusual demands; they demand a disinterested clarification of the facts of the struggle in which one is personally involved, and they demand a sympathetic attitude toward the circumstances of one's opponent. And there is a further demand: a rare faith in the malleability of that opponent.

Satyagraha. Forms of action

"Satyagraha" is a word which connotes the typically Gandhian approach in political and social conflicts. Writing of the South African days Gandhi says that the expression "passive resistance" was not an apt term for the action of the Indians in that country. Gandhi also rejected "paci-

fism." He said that "We had to invent a new term clearly to denote the movement of the Indians in the Transvaal and to prevent its being confused with passive resistance generally so called." [46] *Satya* means "truth," not in the purely theoretical sense of the way in which assertions correspond to reality, but rather in the sense in which we speak of someone as a true friend, in which we think of reality as a form of genuineness. *Agraha* means "grasp," "firmness" or "fixity," and Gandhi says, "Truth (*Satya*) implies love, and firmness (*agraha*) engenders and therefore serves as a synonym for force. I thus began to call the Indian movement 'Satyagraha,' that is to say, the Force which is born of Truth and Love or non-violence, and gave up the use of the phrase 'passive resistance,' in connection with it." [47] These and other general statements by Gandhi, of course, tell us almost nothing. They are too vague and it has become necessary, therefore, to distinguish various meanings of the new word *satyagraha*. According to one interpretation, *satyagraha* is the collective name for just those practical methods used by Gandhi in his campaigns. According to another, *satyagraha* designates the *principles* underlying Gandhi's action; used in this sense, the word is practically a synonym for the concept of "power lying at the base of nonviolent means," or simply for *ahimsa*. Thirdly, it is used as the common name for *all the possible methods* of action, whether exemplified by Gandhi or not, which are in agreement with the teachings of nonviolence; Gandhi's methods, then, would be a subspecies of *satyagraha*—adapted to the special situations in which he worked. It is unfortunate that these three different meanings have been conflated, for considerable confusion inevitably arises in any discussion of *satyagraha*.

Here and there in his writing Gandhi appears to have used the term "satyagraha" in yet another sense; when, for example, he says, "Since *satyagraha* is one of the most powerful methods of direct action, a *satyagrahi* exhausts all other means before he resorts to *satyagraha*." [48] A *satyagrahi* is one who practices *satyagraha,* and we may suppose Gandhi to be saying, "Try by all possible means to come to an understanding with an opponent before you use *satyagraha*." Gandhi would then be using the word in a rather limited way to cover certain far-reaching or extreme forms of direct, nonviolent action in group conflicts, such as "civil disobedience." *Satyagraha* in this fourth sense would thus be a subcategory of *satyagraha* in the third sense. But it is not the sense in which we shall be using the word in what follows.

In the fourth sense, *satyagraha* would refer to certain more or less characteristic procedures in group conflict, but we shall speak here only of a class of phenomena of which *satyagraha* is a component; that is, we shall use *satyagraha* as a common name for procedures in group conflict, without specifying instances. All we shall say is that common to all the procedures we are to call *satyagraha* is that they accord completely, or nearly so, with a specific set of principles, namely the principles constituting the general morality of nonviolence in group conflict. We have already indicated a system made up of such principles. Our use of the word *satyagraha,* then, will agree most nearly with the third sense mentioned above.

Every procedure has its special character. We can put it this way: procedures taken one by one are characteristic of a certain kind of group action, a type of action. The specific character of an individual instance of *satyagraha* procedure is colored by the type of action it exemplifies. On pages 70-71 will be found a short list, a ready-reference, of the kinds of action that *can* be adopted in *satyagraha* campaigns. But especially note this word "can." If a group uses—to mention just one of the procedures in the list—an economic boycott, this in itself does not mean that the action satisfies the requirements for a *satyagraha* campaign. An economic boycott can be undertaken without following at all the principles governing the nonviolent resolution of group conflict, and in such a case would not be *satyagraha* in our sense. Again, any concrete action or campaign is an instance of *satyagraha* if, and only if, (1) those who undertake the action follow the norms of group conflict completely or as nearly completely as possible, and (2) the action falls under one or more of the types given in the definitive list.

Because the list itself has to be regarded as part of the definition of *satyagraha,* the definition becomes rather long. If we wanted a shorter definition, we could try to find what is common to each feature of the list, and formulate it. We would find, however, that we would then end up with a much vaguer expression, one open to so many different interpretations that when we were to explain what we meant, we would have to resort once again to the list. What we would gain in brevity we would lose in self-sufficiency. In the long run, therefore, the longer definition, unwieldy though it may be, cannot be dispensed with.

A most important part of Gandhi's social and political program was the constructive measures it advocated. Take for one example the development of cottage industries and weaving. Gandhi was working toward a society in which, among other things, handicraft would play an important role, a society in which everyone would be satisfactorily employed throughout the year. But home-weaving and handicraft were to function also as a symbol, a symbol, firstly, of the fact that "we Indians are able to help ourselves," and a symbol, secondly, of the feeling against the British laws and regulations which deprived Indians of the opportunity to manufacture their own clothes, and which obliged them to make their own clothes at home or buy them from the British. Thus home-weaving gained far-reaching implications in the struggle against British supremacy. However, since no violation of the law was involved, it became, in principle at least, one feature of a purely constructive program; that is, a positive form of activity in which the revolutionary individual acted as if what he hoped for was already an accomplished fact. This constructive program, as we call it, was something Gandhi laid great store by, not simply in the context of his own campaign, but, more generally, in his efforts toward sustaining a high level of morale, among his followers.

In not treating the constructive program as a *form* of

action, let us not fail to bear in mind, however, that it was by means of the constructive program that every action was to be accomplished. Rather than being merely another instance of action, it was a necessary concomitant of every such instance. As a long-range program, it was to span those intervals of time during which outbreaks of intense conflict might be expected. Individual actions, as Gandhi saw them, were comparatively limited in their aims. The constructive program, on the other hand, was to continue as long as there were powerful tensions in society. It was to consist of a number of reforms and changes in existing social, economic, and political institutions, the aim not being merely to improve those conditions, but to lay a foundation for a new society while the old system continued to exist. These changes were to be effected for their own sake or for the sake of distant aims, such as women's rights, adult education, respect for all religions, and so on. But they were also to have a wider effect; the changes themselves, and the steps taken to bring them about, were to strengthen the self-reliance of the people and their ability to work together toward socially desirable ends. What people take upon themselves to do voluntarily, day by day, in the way of removing social evils, gives them a moral right to take, whenever necessary, a greater part in curing other such evils and in overcoming other such obstacles to constructive reform. When men cooperate, however modestly, toward common ends, they inevitably acquire valuable training for the kind of large-scale cooperation they will require in times of active struggle. Moreover, the self-reliance gained

Satyagraha 67

through a constructive program's stress on self-help, in place of dependence on foreign production and distant markets, can have an important influence on efforts to strengthen connections between different parts of a country. People who were economically self-reliant would be in a better position to form and to preserve freedom in other areas of life, such as politics and law. When the necessities of life are controlled by someone else, that someone else controls more than just the purse-strings; if people are able to satisfy their most elementary needs, to "look after themselves," however, it is far more difficult to dominate and control them. What a constructive program should do is remove the opportunity for economic profiteering and political and economic exploitation, and thereby to eliminate one main cause of international tyranny. Such a program would foster those very qualities that are necessary for, and formed out of, *satyagraha* action, namely, the qualities of self-reliance, independence, and the power of self-decision.

Any *satyagraha* action is based on the *satyagrahi's* two distinct considerations in the face of what opposes him, his attitude to the evil itself and to the person who practices it. In the face of evil itself, the *satyagrahi,* having first tried to cleanse *himself* of it, is duty-bound to show his opponent in what respects his action is evil, and then to try to convince him to mend his ways. If talking to the man gets him nowhere, the *satyagrahi* must persist in his appeal, must try to affect a change of heart by taking upon himself any burden of suffering or pain that may result from the conflict between himself and his opponent. Then secondly, the *satyagrahi* must deny all cooperation with the evil-doer and convince everyone, especially the evil-doer's close associates, to do likewise. According to Gandhi's view, it is the willing cooperation of underlings that makes oppression and injustice possible; a refusal to cooperate, therefore, should bring an effective end to such things. This denial of cooperation can, of course, be manifested in one or more types of action. In a particular *satyagraha* campaign the stress may lie on either of the *satyagrahi*'s two considerations, that is of dealing with evil itself and with those who perpetrate it; sometimes both may apply equally. But it is against the background of this twofold attitude, and against the background of the principles of *satyagraha* that one must view the different kinds of action adopted in the campaigns themselves. Seen in this perspective, the use, say, of an economic boycott, can appear in quite a different light from what would otherwise be the case.

Gandhi thought that the forms of action could be so arranged that they would become increasingly stringent and forceful as the struggle between a *satyagraha* group and its opponents developed: more stringent—that is, more far-reaching, or extreme—in the sense of demanding qualitatively greater sacrifice and suffering on both sides; more forceful, in the sense of generating greater power and effectiveness.

There is no reason to provide a detailed list of all the appropriate kinds of action. For that there are other sources, not least the reader's own imagination.[49] Generally, however, it is plain enough that the kinds of action concerned, if they are to be used in *satyagraha* campaigns and, hence, are in agreement with the system of principles, can take on a character quite different from that of actions in ordinary struggles. We have only to think, for example, of Gandhi's unusual demand that all documents relevant to a conflict be placed before all of the antagonists.

What follows is a classification of the kinds of action which can be used in *satyagraha* campaigns, provided, of course, that they are so employed that the principles of nonviolence are upheld:

MILD ACTION

Negotiations

Arbitration

Agitation (without breaking the law)

Demonstrations of various kinds

(without breaking the law)

SEVERE ACTION

(Actions in this class are also understood

as not to involve breaking the law)

Ordinary, limited strikes, of short duration

General strike   Economic boycott

Social boycott

EXTREME ACTION

Fasting

Emigration

Extensive institutional non-cooperation Civil disobedience[50] (Including breaking laws, but only such as are found ethically reprehensible)

Systematic disobedience (Including breaking laws which individually may not be at fault, but are part of the system struggled against)

Parallel government   Total disobedience

Classification along other dimensions is, of course, needed. The way of classifying action from "mild" to "extreme" was, however, often used by Gandhi himself, and it must for that reason alone, if no other, be viewed as a most important one.

To agitation in a wider sense belong the special forms of action used, for instance, by pickets during strikes. However, if the law forbids meetings and certain kinds of propaganda, this would become a more severe kind of action which would involve breaking the law. Closely related to agitation, at least outwardly, would be demonstrations in the form of marches, banner-waving, placard-carrying, and so on. Examples have already been mentioned: the Indian women's march on the mines to convince the miners to go on strike, and the miners' march into the Transvaal as a demonstration against a number of laws and restrictions, especially against economic and racial discrimination.

Simply in order to get a clear view of all these forms of action, we have made a distinction between forms that involve breaking laws and conventions, and those that do not. Demonstration and agitation are relegated to the latter. But, of course, this classification is not an entirely adequate one; we can easily find situations in which any demonstration or agitation would involve breaking laws or conventions. However, we may note that in such cases the conflict is inevitably aggravated. More restricted actions may involve greater risks, perhaps, for those who perform them, but the possibilities of success are also greater.[51]

In his *The Future of Mankind,* Karl Jaspers arrives at a negative conclusion regarding nonviolent action.[52] But this is at least in part due to a strange identification of *power* with *force* or *compulsion.* He is quite right in maintaining that no methods can succeed in politics without the use of power. But he seems to infer from this that therefore no movement can succeed *without* the use of force or compulsion. From the correct observation that it is impossible for nonviolence to succeed without the use of power, he infers that it cannot succeed at all!

The distinction between compulsion and conversion is important: if a fast by Gandhi leads to his opponent's "giving in" on the grounds of the immorality of causing the death of another, but without any genuine belief in Gandhi's proposals, then the case is one which we would properly describe as "compulsion on moral grounds." The opponent is compelled to give in against his will, and if Gandhi *makes use of* the opponent's moral convictions in order to reach his goal, then he makes use of compulsion or force.

Gandhi was, of course, against such compulsion: "I

repeat what I have said before—nothing is to be done under pressure of the fast. I have observed before that things done under pressure of a fast have been undone after the fast is over. If any such thing happens it would be a tragedy of the highest degree." [53] But if Gandhi *convinces* an opponent through fasting, then he has used power and not compulsion. As long as we fail to distinguish power from force and violence, the conclusions of Jaspers (and other critics) hold: that is, that Gandhi, in his morality, far from doing away with violence and compulsion, merely finds another name and place for it.

However, even if this conclusion were true, there is a vast difference between warfare, say, and moral pressure. What is achieved by moral pressure is not dependent on the maintenance of that pressure for its continuance, nor will people outside the conflict be directly injured by it. Violence, as in the use of napalm bombs on enemy towns and settlements, is something quite different from the exercise of moral pressure.

In the English language it is possible, and normal, to distinguish power from violence. The confusion of the two that we find in Jaspers, and many other German philosophers, is perhaps not unconnected with a general failure to distinguish, in the German language, between *Macht* and *Gewalt*. Jaspers says that *"Politik ihrem Wesen nach"* is *"Umgang mit der Gewalt,"* and, as long as we leave the expression *"Gewalt"* imprecise, this statement of his can only be misleading.[54]

An important tenet in the contemporary political philosophy of "power" or "strength" maintains that violent exertion of power is not just one of many ways of exerting power, but "power," "violence" and "threats of violence" are near synonyms. Another current of thought, equally important, bases itself on a concept of power akin to Spinoza's. The power (potentia) of a being (individual, state, or group) is its ability to act out of its own individuality, spontaneously, and without compulsion from another. Nevertheless, when one being acts under the *influence* of another, or, more generally, when it is stimulated by something outside itself, it does not *thereby* exhibit its impotence. If it is raining, for example, and I put up my umbrella, it would be an expression of my impotence if I did so simply because it was a generally accepted social principle that one should avoid getting wet, even though I personally enjoyed a good soaking. But if, by nature, I dislike getting wet, the use of an umbrella to ward off the rain would be an expression of my power—my ability to act from my own nature. The rain influences my action, but it does not coerce or compel me. In the same way, if an opponent appeals to a moral principle and convinces me in spite of myself of the goodness of something, I can still do as my opponent suggests without thereby expressing any impotence.

Despite his theoretical reservations, however, Jaspers holds that Gandhi pointed in the right direction in the present world crisis. This favorable opinion stems from the fact that Gandhi anchored his method in the suprapolitical: "Today we face the question of how to escape from physical force, and from war, lest we all perish by the atom bomb. Gandhi, in word and deed, gives the true answer: Only a suprapolitical force can bring political salvation." [55]

When huge numbers of people are engaged in a nonviolent struggle, things easily degenerate into violence if they are not properly organized. Gandhi therefore wished to organize struggles through elite groups. But he found himself unable to organize on a national scale these groups, the so-called "nonviolent brigades" which were to cover all of the centers of unrest in India. The idea was that, by contributing to the common good in their immediate surroundings, these nonviolent workers would acquire the moral stature and good-will to combat warring factions and hooligans. In the event of a bloody uprising in any centers of unrest, they were to go into action and pacify those who were on the point of using arms. Furthermore, when mass action was under way, the brigades were supposed to place themselves among the crowds and step in at the moment when any disorderly factions got out of hand and started threatening their opponents. But Gandhi quickly discovered the enormous difference between, on the one hand, personally abstaining from violence and, on the other, throwing oneself into a crisis so as to hinder the use of violence by others. While thousands could conduct themselves entirely without violence in a situation in which they were being struck with clubs, or provoked in some other equally brutal manner, there were only a few who, themselves in safety, could be relied upon to move into a center of violence and actively try to prevent bloodshed.

An especially dangerous situation arose in the large

cities, areas of rapidly increasing industrialization, for there the poor, out of work and generally unsettled, collected again and again to roam the streets, and to act in a more and more chaotic and disruptive way. These elements were, of course, very hard to influence. The solution that Gandhi decided upon was for *satyagraha* brigades to work, over a period of time, in specific districts and get to know the trouble-makers. By having men whom these trouble-makers could completely trust go amongst them and thereby win their confidence, Gandhi hoped to influence them and to keep them from the kind of violence that would eventually lead to massacres.

In summary, then, we may say that Gandhi felt that his experiments with *satyagraha* justified the trust he put in its methods in solving group conflicts. On the one hand, we have his own particular experiences; on the other, certain of his general hypotheses, together with some of his general statements. The statements and hypotheses themselves, if acceptable, would allow us to predict quite generally the fact that *satyagraha* can achieve significant results. The choice of the word "significant" rather than, say, "unlimited" is made advisedly—Gandhi foresaw no unqualified success. As we said before, *satyagraha* here is so defined that an action which meets only approximately the principles of nonviolent action can still be designated *satyagraha*. If we required of a *satyagraha* action that it satisfy fully and exactly all of the specified conditions, such as the absence of hatred and so on, we could never accept Gandhi's statement that he had practiced, and not merely intended, *satyagraha*. He himself felt that he had never achieved a completely nonviolent action and we have no reason whatever to doubt the justness of his own verdict. Nonetheless, the degree to which his actions accorded with the principles he set himself was certainly very high, and this fact is sufficient to justify our claim that Gandhi was a *satyagrahi*—that is, one who actually used *satyagraha*.

What happens, we can ask, when a *satyagrahi* keeps to a high level of *satyagraha* but his opponent does not give in, or only with the greatest difficulty is persuaded to withhold his opposition? Consistent application of the doctrine of progressive *satyagraha* might then lead to the adoption of severe and possibly extreme forms of action. It is interesting to note here that when non-extreme forms do not lead to positive results, the Gandhian principles require one to proceed to the establishment of a parallel government. Leo Tolstoy's teaching of nonviolence and his morality of nonviolence, however, are allied to a less ambitious trust in man's susceptibility to influence, and thus to a less confident belief in the forms of action adopted by Gandhi. It is characteristic also of Tolstoy and his adherents that they kept themselves as far removed from the State as possible; we can see that part of Tolstoy's teaching was a comprehensive form of anarchism. And among Indian moralists before Gandhi a similar pessimism is also to be found. By far the greatest majority of them were not *karmayogi*, i.e., not men of action, but men who withheld themselves from the business and turmoil of life in order to live lives unmarked by violence.

Some people may say that optimism about the outcome of nonviolent action is not an essential part of Gandhi's philosophy or moral teaching. But then they are surely identifying moral teaching with abstract science, just as one can, if one chooses, identify astronomy with those mathematical formulae which describe a body's action under the force of gravity, rather than with an astronomer's theories and descriptions of individual planets and other heavenly bodies. Taken in this way, astronomy is only a branch of mathematics. No one will doubt, however, that astronomy does include a reference to the factual universe as well as to abstract generalities. In the same way, a morality built up systematically must contain references to particular actions, real concrete possibilities for such action, and the probable results of such actions. Unless moral philosophy is thus made concrete, we would be forced to resort to an attitude which allows two widely different ethical statements to be interpreted identically when it comes to particular performances in the world, or, conversely, which would allow identical statements of moral principle to lead to diametrically opposed consequences. However, both the doctrine governing the forms of action, and the view about their effects, are genuine components of Gandhi's moral philosophy, and hence also of his political philosophy. To pessimists he said: "Have you tried? I have, and it works."

Part Three

GANDHI'S POLITICAL MORALITY
COMPARED TO THE POLITICAL
MORALITIES OF LUTHER, HOBBES,
NIETZSCHE, AND TOLSTOY

Luther and Gandhi

We now have a fairly clear, if not wholly complete, picture of Gandhi's ideas and intentions. Let us compare them, then, with what we know of the ideas and intentions of some other men who have lent their minds to the same problems of conflict. Such a comparison can do more than to put the Gandhian philosophy in clearer perspective, it can also tell us just where the comparison and contrast of different philosophies can significantly be made. It is the failure to see such possibilities that often gives rise to hasty claims and endless arguments between those critics of a tradition who betray a superficial grasp of its originator's views, and those supporters of the tradition who seek to defend themselves by delving among the treasured *obiter dicta* of their master for some view less vulnerable to criticism. A notable case in point are the arguments about group conflict between Lutherans and non-Lutherans, and they provide as good a starting-point as any to develop further our ideas about Gandhi.

We find Martin Luther's views on group conflict in his doctrine of the two "regiments," or "realms," the spiritual and the worldly. The worldly realm, which is in a sense the kingdom of evil, and which exists only because there is evil in man, is the world of militarism. God has laid the world of evil beneath the sword, as men have put wild beasts in chains.

However, Luther's two regiments cannot be straightforwardly identified with the Church and worldly power. The Swedish theologian Anders Nygren puts Luther's view in this way:

In the worldly regiment God will maintain justice and peace, and the means he uses in this regiment are power and the sword. In both the one and the other kingdom he uses men as his servants.

Princes, soldiers, and those who are subjected to imprisonment, are all servants of God. Nygren goes on:

Through the gospel God rules his spiritual kingdom, forgives sins, justifies and sanctifies. But in no way has He thereby made the worldly regiment out-dated, or done away with it. In its domain the worldly regiment shall rule with power and the sword. If one tries to inject the gospel into its regime, then one commits a two-fold sin, and so will be doubly punished. Primarily one corrupts

Gandhi's political morality 82

the gospel; but in addition to this one harms and corrupts the world.[1]

The gospel is not to be used in order to eliminate militarism, for that would be to corrupt the gospel. Luther himself says:

If someone will rule this world according to the gospel and abrogate all worldly justice and the sword. . . . What will he accomplish thereby? He will turn loose the wild, evil beasts from their bonds and chains.

The substance, then, of Luther's view seems to be that if one interferes with the worldly regiment, the very few good people who do live according to the gospel will be killed. In his treatise, *Ob Kriegsleute auch im seelingen Stande sein können,* (Whether the soldier can be considered a Christian), Luther says:

Therefore God also sets the sword on high, which obeys his will, and does not want man to say or to believe that man has discovered it or invented it. For the hand which uses this sword and kills is no longer a human hand, but God's hand, and not man but God hangs, breaks on the wheel, delivers, kills, and makes war. All the work and the justice are his.

For our own purposes, Luther's separate points can be listed as follows:

1. He began with the attitude that relations between peoples would continue for some time amidst war and other violence organized by one state for use against other states.

2. He felt that political affairs, for example, constitutional matters, would remain essentially as they were in his age. The individual's defense against the practices of princes would be to behave as if the princes had absolute power. Defense against autocracy, in other words, could not generally be considered at all, or could be considered only very indirectly.

3. Luther assumed that treatment of law-breakers would also continue as it was in the 1500s. Such an assumption gave legal sanction to maltreatment and torture, and condoned the infliction of punishment on children and on the mentally ill. In the passage quoted above, for example, Luther mentions breaking on the wheel, a form of torture which was followed by death. "Good men," as he says, must be protected against "wild animals" by any means. And there cannot be any doubt, according to Luther, about who are good and who evil.

4. Even if any given set of administrative institutions in a state cannot be wholly *identified* with God's worldly kingdom in that state, their connection is nonetheless so close that any change in the institutions is tantamount to a change in God's own regime. Thoroughgoing reforms must be taken, therefore, to be expressions of a dissatisfaction with God. The close connection of God's own regime to the persons who rule the state, moreover, makes it the duty of any ordinary person to obey the ruling powers. But there are, for Luther, certain interesting exceptions. One *does* have the right to disobey the ruling classes, but to do this, one must be a so-called "Wundermensch" (miracle-man), that is, must have a special commission from God to go

against worldly power. Such commissions Luther considered to be very rare. But he thought of *himself* as one such *Wundermensch* when he nailed his theses to the church door.

5. Luther divided men, as we have said, into the good and the evil, and did not count much on the possibility of the good exerting any positive influence upon the evil, or of their effecting any other great change. The good men, the real Christians, were, according to Luther, few in number, perhaps no more than one in a thousand.

6. Evil men, he felt, would not flinch from exterminating the good men if the worldly regiment did not use force. Luther compared evil men to wolves who would devour the sheep if the sheep were not protected. This situation would be especially serious if there were a thousand wolves to each sheep! It is no more than reasonable under such circumstances to sanction any imaginable means of defense, especially since the use of brutal means by good men does not, according to Luther, make them any less good. And their defense would not be of an idea, but simply of the good.

7. Princes and ruling powers are more or less superior, morally, to the masses. Those who have become rulers may be assumed to have certain powers which their subjects lack.

8. There are two moralities, individual morality and the morality of rulers, or rather, common morality and superior morality. "Thou shalt not kill" holds for the commonalty, but not for the ruling order. At times, however, the commonalty may kill; "Thou shalt not

kill" and "Thou shalt not torture" need not hold for them either; as servants of the ruling order, they do have the right and sometimes the duty to kill, but not on their own initiative.

9. The morality of the ruling order follows the law of justice, that of the subject follows the law of love. However, this is not the case in situations where commoners carry out the wishes of the ruling order. In such cases, in war for example, to follow the law of love would be to rebel against God.

Much of the harshness of Luther's teaching is thought to be inseparable from the spirit of his age. It is therefore considered unjust to compare him to such a man as Gandhi, who lived in an age which had more or less rejected the idea of the innate goodness of the ruling classes. Let us remember, however, that there are still people today who support Luther's teaching, accepting even its harshest features; there is, therefore, more than academic interest in comparing Gandhi with Luther.

Gandhi and Luther both condemned, on moral grounds, the political and personal conduct of their age. But Gandhi thought it possible, nay, desirable, to effect radical changes, and should such changes require the elimination of certain institutions, so much the worse, he felt, for these institutions. Institutions themselves were, for Gandhi, far from divine. War, and the threat of war, were, for instance, bad institutions. The structure of society needed to be changed, but it was not necessary to be a superman or a *Wundermensch* in order to oppose ruling authority.

Gandhi's political morality

Gandhi wanted a revolution, but not violence. He saw how Hinduism had become decadent, and he wanted to purify it. He considered the original caste system to have a valuable core, but that it had grown corrupt over the centuries. Such an institution was not to be eliminated, but restored. In short, even if there were much evil in the world, even if human institutions were never perfect, passivity in the face of evil was altogether unjustifiable.

For Luther, matters stood quite differently. No actually existing institution could, in principle, be bad, for God had created it. War was such an institution. Although those who acted for such an institution could be evil, as when a ruler conducted an evil war, the repetition of this evil could, according to Luther, only be avoided by the ruler's being converted and becoming a true Christian. If a Christian were to start an evil war, he would not be a true Christian. It is individual human beings that do good or evil. In sum, evil-doers may be done away with, but not institutions.

Gandhi's view was diametrically opposed to this. In the anti-British campaign, for instance, the Prince of Wales, as a representative of the ruling order, was boycotted, but as a man and an individual he had to be accorded every respect; neither he nor the opponents of the boycott were to suffer any injury. While Luther thought that since the office a man held was inviolable, and that the tenure of that office afforded such a man the personal rights of respect and nonviolation, Gandhi felt it was the opponent's person (and not just his body) which was inviolable, and only his acts as a representative of a ruling order as something which could be systematically opposed. Authoritarian or totalitarian forms of government are not, after all, essential; "princes" of the kind Luther speaks about may have been an evil, but they were not a necessary evil. That war is an evil and also an institution is no argument in favor of war. Luther seems to have ruled out the possibility of non-oppressive alternatives to the institutions of war and dictatorship.

As for justice and imprisonment, Gandhi felt not only that maltreatment and torture must cease, but also that imprisonment must be abolished. No distinction, said Gandhi, should be made between the law of justice and the law of love. There exists only one morality, the morality of love, and according to this morality all people, commoners and rulers alike, stand on the same level.

Furthermore, from a moral point of view, no man can act for another man: if the hangman is to justify himself, he must do so only within his own personal morality; his role or function provides him with no excuses or justification. The basis of Gandhi's teaching in connection with group conflict is that men, wherever they have dealings with one another, must meet and interact as individual persons, not as representatives, functionaries, or underlings. Every man is more than the sum of his functions, and what he cannot excuse or justify in terms of his totality is not to be excused or justified in terms of those functions.

All men are susceptible to influence, but not, indeed, to influence by just anyone. The more a man has developed, the greater the possibilities of his being susceptible to a good influence. Gandhi's view is that which is usually summed up as "perfectionism" or "meliorism": man can always change: "however debased or fallen he may be, [he] has in him the capacity of rising to the greatest height ever attained by any human being." [2] How far he climbs depends on what people, and through them, what groups he comes to be influenced by.

Furthermore, an action may be good or bad; not so a man. If we talk about good and bad persons, our statements must be understood in reference to the actions and attitudes of persons, not to the persons themselves. A man may *behave* like a lamb or like a wolf, but in either case he remains a man.

This point is essential to Gandhi's *satyagraha,* for that procedure would certainly be a tragically vain one if one did not first believe that one's opponent could be influenced. If we believe, on the other hand, that there is practically no way in which the opposition is open to influence, that there is as little hope of personal influence as there is, for instance, of inducing a squid to refrain from emptying its ink-sac, then we should simply accept as a fact of nature that men will defend their biological existence by any means available, blind to influence, blind to argument, blind to morality. It would certainly then be both foolish and foolhardy to act as though we expected otherwise.

There is now a tendency to criticize Luther's secular view in something of an unfair way. We should remember, however, that Luther wanted above all to bring himself into agreement with the Bible and that he was also a member of a powerful tradition, a tradition of pessimism about the world and about earthly existence. This tradition is one that we can trace to the earliest Christianity.

We can mention in this connection, moreover, Albert Schweitzer's interpretation of Christianity. Johan Hygen states that as far as his views on the New Testament are concerned, Schweitzer represents the so-called "consistent eschatology":

The religion of Jesus, according to Schweitzer, is not a religion which wishes to remake the world, but a religion which lives in expectation of the world's end. Its view of the world is pessimistic. Along with this interpretation of the earliest Christianity, Schweitzer maintains that the increasing dominance of the optimistic element came in at the Renaissance as a result of our somewhat changed attitude to the Christianity of the first centuries. It was a structural change. Indeed Schweitzer goes so far as to say that in exchanging optimism for pessimism Christianity lost its original essence.[3]

Since early Christians expected the end of the world to come any day, there was little reason for them, downtrodden as they were, to try to change the Roman Empire and its institutions. They might attempt to convert an occasional member of the ruling order, but what would be the point in trying to change institutions just as the world was coming to an end? If one believes, however, the end of the world to be some way off, one's interest in institutions and the possibility of putting them to rights, may grow considerably. But Luther, in trying to retrace the progress of his Church back to early Christianity, unquestioningly took over the traditional view of the imminent end of the world.

We referred above to some of the tacit assumptions in Luther's teaching: assumptions, among other things, about the immutability of the worldly regime. If Luther's social ideas are to provide us with any guidance today, we must believe that Luther made use of these assumptions about the worldly regime quite consciously. On the other hand, we may well doubt that he went at all deeply into worldly or social questions. His main wish, after all, was to be a guide to his own age, and we do him an injustice if we see him as trying to provide basic truths of sociology valid for all time. Most theologians recognize the uncertainty of determining what Luther's views would be if he lived today. For instance, there is some controversy about how to interpret the expression "just war," which Luther used to designate wars of which he approved. A just war has been traditionally interpreted as one that is declared by a country's legal government, but this interpretation is now looked on as being as much a product of his age as was the Augsburg Confession. We cannot argue, that is, that Luther's views would imply his advocacy of nuclear warfare today. His position in contemporary controversy in this respect is still, and must remain, an open one.

According to their interpretations of Luther and of the evangelical Lutheran faith, most Lutheran theologians have felt that both the man and the faith are at a very great distance from Gandhian political morality. Nevertheless, there has always been among Lutherans a current of "nonviolence." In the Norwegian (Lutheran) State Church, for example, there is a widespread feeling that attitudes have changed a good deal since Luther's day, and that the sixteenth article of the Augsburg Confession provides an adequate basis for Gandhian-like decisions on matters of politics, even in the world as it is today.

The words of the Lutheran creed cannot be given a meaning which would totally exclude sympathy with Gandhi's political morality; but then neither can it be given one which excludes sympathy with a diametrically opposed morality. However, the more interesting question that today occupies theologians on this subject is that which asks: how far have we correctly understood the Bible itself in what it says about violence, strife, and the waging of war?

Hobbes and Gandhi

If consistency and lucidity were the prime measures of philosophical stature, then Thomas Hobbes would have to be considered one of the greatest philosophers of all time. His philosophy, conveyed with such admirable clarity, accepts a "materialist" view of the structure of the world, and in the field of morals an "egoistic" form of hedonism; that is, it holds that man, throughout his life, never desists from seeking what is good for himself. According to Hobbes, therefore, man is constantly striving after pleasure and the avoidance of pain; this process is an unceasing and inevitable one.

He also holds, however, that the achievement of these

ends depends upon the rational use of the available means. In thinking about the future, that is, man forms rational hypotheses about the conditions and institutions which will afford him greater pleasure than pain. But, when aroused, men often find it hard to listen to the counsel of reason, and in actual conflict, where self-interest calls very clearly for rational procedures, they tend to become especially excitable and unreasonable. This accounts for those unfortunate actions which have self-interest as their motive but self-destruction as their result. Thus war enters the arena of human affairs, not as the expression of rationally and coolly calculated self-interest, but as the infringement of that principle which later came to be called "enlightened self-interest."

How, we should ask, do wars come about? They come about because, when we pursue pleasure or joy ignorantly, short-sightedly, and without sufficient self-awareness, we inevitably come into conflict with other people who are similarly occupied. These others constitute an obstacle to our own pleasure, and it becomes necessary to dispose of them. Minor conflicts start this way, and campaigns to organize support for minor causes follow soon thereafter; wars on a massive scale are the natural and ultimate result.[3]

Since war, to say the least, gives rise to unpleasant feelings, and also to sorrow and uncertainty in the intervals between wars, and since there is little worse than constant sorrow and uncertainty, the highest principle, in Hobbes's view, is: *Seek peace and preserve it.* To this he adds: if you do not succeed in maintaining peace, then go to war and use every means to ensure success.[4]

Though it is this last point that people are careful to stress in presenting Hobbes's views, there is much in Hobbes that would seem to indicate that for him a decisive, perhaps *the* decisive, problem was that of obtaining a lasting peace. In his view, war continues only because of the inadequacy of human vision, because of man's failure to live rationally according to self-knowledge.

What connection can we see here with Gandhi? First of all, Hobbes seems to think that if we believe our rational faculties not to be strong enough to preclude conflict, or to resolve it in a rational way, then not only is it reasonable to prepare for the eventuality of war but to do so is even quite compatible with a policy that aims at eliminating war. Gandhi, however, thinks that the cool and deliberate decision to act on an assumption of weakness and irrationality is incompatible with sincere efforts to overcome such weakness and irrationality, and, in addition, leads us all at last to suspect that a rational solution can not even be envisaged. If irrationality is openly accepted in moments of comparative peace, we can hardly entertain any serious hopes for rationality in a time of crisis. Gandhi assumes, then, that it is impossible to struggle wholeheartedly for peace and at the same time retain the means of war—we cannot meet our opponent in any truly friendly spirit if we always carry a knife in our pocket "just in case." He will almost certainly see through our pretenses and discover the uncertainty and hypocrisy which they hide. The knife, as an ultimate means, will always loom larger in his estimation of our good-will, than the conciliatory words and winning smile with which we confront him at our "friendly talks."

Apart from these differences between their views on "pre-war" attitudes, Hobbes and Gandhi differ also about the results of war. Hobbes appears to have believed that the bad effects of warlike acts were confined to the fact that they diminished the chances of success in future efforts to maintain a lasting peace, whereas Gandhi held that warlike acts have decisively negative results of their own, whatever the outcome of the war.

Without discussing the differences in their metaphysical postulates, we can discover a crucial enough difference between Hobbes's and Gandhi's ideas on group conflict. It would be very difficult, however, to undertake a precise and detailed comparison, for Hobbes himself never developed his ideas far enough to specify particular forms of action in conflict.

This brings us to a significant feature of our study: *a point by point comparison of Gandhi with central western thinkers simply cannot be made, because the latter do not make systematic reference to group conflict within the frame of a more inclusive doctrine.*

The demand for openness (no secret documents, private bargaining, etc.) and the delimitation of definite goals, is itself sufficient, of course, to distinguish Gandhi's actions from those which seem similar but which are operated within a framework in which violence is condoned. The framework, that is, determines the character of each part of the doctrine. The particular forms of action, for example, negotiation, arbitration, strikes, and so on, take on different aspects depending on the system of principles adopted in employing them.

Why, as a matter of fact, did Hobbes not go into detail

about the possibilities of nonviolent means in group conflict? One tentative answer might be: he had no grounds for assuming that organized violence and threats of organized violence could be eliminated or even constrained in his time by consistently applied nonviolent methods. Hobbes lacked, in other words, an incentive and a precedent for developing theories like that of *satyagraha*.

To return now to Gandhi: first, to his optimistic view that it is good *Realpolitik* to count on the possibility of reaching nonviolent solutions to group conflicts, secondly, to his imaginativeness in the matter of finding suitable forms for the manifestation of a struggle, and thirdly, to his sceptical attitude toward the idea that, at a pinch, when all other methods have misfired, one can obtain by war what one has tried but failed to obtain by peace.

For Hobbes, just as for Gandhi, ethical questions are not autonomous. Hobbes takes as his starting-point an assumed natural law which says that man seeks pleasure and endeavors to avoid pain. It is possible, of course, to develop a theory, based on such a law, which would run entirely parallel to the Gandhian theory of group conflict. Hobbes's aim, the establishment of lasting peace, is in fact an acceptable object in every way for activities of the Gandhian kind. In principle, one can in fact incorporate nonviolence within the framework of any system that already contains a principle about securing lasting peace. Questions, however, about the significance of this principle arise when we investigate a system's further principles and hypotheses.

Hobbes's determinism did not prevent him from recognizing that men can *choose* between different means to their own "felicity"; there is no principle, therefore, preventing one from constructing a morality on the Hobbesian basis, with, for example, the tenet: "Seek the maximum self-preservation" as the highest norm. Hobbes did, as a matter of fact, consider self-preservation to be the end served by pleasure and pain, and from this it is not far to the acceptance of "self-realization" as the highest aim. The distance can, in fact, be measured by a comparison of the extremely confined ego Hobbes talks about in his egoistic or psychological hedonism, or the self he presupposes in the doctrine of self-preservation, with that of the broad "I" or "Self" which Gandhi saw as fundamentally identical to all life.

The fact, however, that most of us feel that Gandhi and Hobbes stand worlds apart may not be unconnected with the stamp of religious intensity which Gandhi's activity bore, and with his tendency to clothe his principles in the garb of "duty." Reduced, however, to their systematic forms and with the special coloring of their particular appeals removed, the differences between the philosophies of the two men are much less evident. In any case, the tradition started by Hobbes and others in European political philosophy does not clearly contradict Gandhi's, simply because it does not comprise any specific ethics and methodology of group struggle.

Nietzsche and Gandhi

It is a simple matter to set Friedrich Nietzsche and Mohandas Gandhi in opposition to one another; in fact it may seem almost too easy to be interesting. Nietzsche's views on war and his expressed admiration for Napoleon and other great warriors of the past would surely seem to make the contrast with Gandhi an absolute, and, therefore, a useless, one. In so far as Nietzsche, in fact, contributed nothing to political morality, neither directly nor indirectly, it indeed does no justice to the great philosopher-poet to enlist him into the ranks of political philosophers. Nevertheless, the attempt to do so has been made, and it might therefore be well to clarify those points at which Nietzsche's views seem vulnerable to such wayward interpretations as we find, for example, in Sorel and the National Socialists; and of course it is at times useful to see just where comparisons *cannot* be made.

Consider first Nietzsche's views on war. How are we to interpret his approval of war, violence, and cruelty? There are two traditional interpretations of Nietzsche, the external-literal and the internal-symbolic. The literalists take Nietzsche at his word: wars can, generally speaking, be good things. And yet, according to Nietzsche, contemporary wars, including the Franco-Prussian War, were inglorious affairs. The Prussian "victory" over France was no victory at all, and the "Era of Bismarck" was an era of "Germans made stupid!" [5] Was the only fault of contemporary warfare its ingloriousness? Would wars, shorn of their accidental ignobility, and adorned with a few of the necessary positive characteristics, be quite all right, be in fact desirable? The answer must be a firm No. Even if Nietzsche, in his conversation and diaries, *had* shown enthusiasm for contemporary wars and violence, because they served the repression of the physically and economically weak, the validity of the external-literal interpretation of Nietzsche's works would still not be established at all. Himself a man of precarious health, Nietzsche showed little inclination to engage personally in political controversy or group struggle.[6] It is without undue exaggeration that M. P. Nicolas could say, "Neither directly nor by implication, neither in practice nor in theory, was Nietzsche ever concerned with politics." [7]

It would require too much space to launch into a detailed justification here of the internal-symbolic interpretation of terms in Nietzsche's works such as "war," "cruelty" and "violence" and to define them in terms of inner struggles, or in terms of conflicts fought in the mind by those concerned with their own weakness. Suffice it to say that Nietzsche seems clearly to have conceived himself to be continually declaring and waging "wars." Of his book, *Human, All too Human,* he writes that it constituted "a hundred-fold declaration of war." He fought established Christianity with the same intensity as did Kierkegaard. "It is now that we shall need warriors", he remarked *after* the immense Prussian victory at Sedan. These and other sayings show how he used a martial vocabulary which omitted entirely any reference to international relations. Attempts, therefore, to construct a political morality or a theory of group conflict on the basis of Nietzsche's writings would seem doomed to failure. Comparison with Gandhi at this level, then, is impossible.[8]

But what about Nietzsche's noble warriors? Are they anything like Gandhi's *satyagrahi?* Those warriors are courageous, honest, and they are masters of *open* combat; they make sacrifices, take responsibilities upon themselves, and never extol suffering. They are truth-seekers, "free-spirits"; their personal *"Weltanschauung"* is the arbiter of all their decisions; they neither evade issues, shun conflicts, nor flee from fearful, even deadly, consequences, but hold their ground come what may.

Gandhi expected similar qualities of his *satyagrahi;* in fact he has often been criticized for the harshness and cruelty of his demands. His admiration for the proud but warlike Pathans and his criticism of the weakness of some Hindus seem to reflect an uncompromisingly "strong" and militant attitude.

No systematic comparison of Gandhi and Nietzsche, however, is possible even in this area. The problems involved in interpreting the two men are vastly different. Nietzsche, perhaps intentionally, never makes clear when he is trying to convey something in a highly suggestive but not fully literal way, and when he intends people to be able to point to some sentence and say, "There, that is what Nietzsche thinks about it." Where Nietzsche, in other words, talks at us through an opaque screen of inspiration, Gandhi takes care to avoid metaphors, and utters the most direct statements in the simplest of prose.

Furthermore, if we can talk at all of Nietzsche's system of morality, it is clear that we can say that it lacks any account of how to proceed, or what to expect, in particular situations. His statements about actual occurrences and his more specific references to persons are confined to remarks about, *inter alia,* wars, Jews, the British, the French, and so forth. The generality of such references lends support to what seems the correct way of interpreting Nietzsche, a way that implies that these general statements are less straightforward references to real instances than illustrations of aspects of the great struggle man must have with himself if he is not to be destroyed. The key, it would seem, to much of Nietzsche's discussion of "war" in *Also sprach Zarathustra* is to be found in the statement: "Your highest thought shall they let me bid you and cry out: Man is something that shall be overcome." [9] The picture we are given of man is of a weak and cowardly being, passive, compromising, dishonest, evasive and foolish; a being which feels compassion but refuses to commit itself to the hazards of moral action. The man Nietzsche would conquer is a self-effacing, un-self-realized, man. Self-realization is a matter of self-conquering, in so far as the "little self" must be overcome. This notion of annihilating the weakness of man and thereby admitting a greater self which has no known bounds, is perhaps the main principle that emerges from any prolonged acquaintance with the works of Nietzsche.

However, it is impossible, at least at the present time, to explicate any further principles in his philosophy which would allow us to compare the Nietzschian system with others. And for the connection with Gandhi, we can say at least that both men undeniably support some values in common. We can say little more.

Tolstoy and Gandhi

Leo Tolstoy was Gandhi's great inspiration in the latter's efforts to evolve a theory of politics that could accommodate his moral system. In some ways Tolstoy was the more radical and uncompromising of the two, especially with regard to opposing the powers that be. In specifying very clearly how the authorities should be approached in an actual conflict, Gandhi expressed his belief that there are times when a good cause can be supported by working with the authorities, even though they might be responsible for violence and oppression. Tolstoy's belief seems to have been, on the contrary, that a good cause can never be supported in this way. In one important respect, then, Gandhi appears to have differed from his main source of inspiration.

In his detailed accounts of the cruelties inflicted on the peasants by the Tsarist authorities, Tolstoy gives free rein to his indignation. There is never a hint of any possibility of future cooperation with the perpetrators of such terrible violence. He writes as though he intended to convey to his readers a mood of hatred not just for the institutions, but for all of their representatives as well.

With Gandhi it was quite otherwise. He presents the assaults and injuries suffered by himself and his followers, in such a way that we are roused more to sorrow than to hatred, and more to a willingness to fight the causes of animosity and distrust than to a desire to wreak vengeance on the offenders. Gandhi had a rare gift for the vehement condemnation of an act without condemning its agent. His unwillingness to make personal accusations even extended to fanatics and terrorists, since even they were to be regarded as potential fellow-workers. No one could be written off; no one was beyond redemption. The tone of Gandhi's writings differs from that of Tolstoy's as the mental attitude of a builder does from that of a destroyer.

Romain Rolland, in his book on Gandhi, written in 1924, said: "With Gandhi everything is nature—modest, simple, pure—while all his struggles are hallowed by religious serenity, whereas with Tolstoy everything is proud revolt against pride, hatred against hatred, passion against passion. Everything in Tolstoy is violence, even his doctrine of non-violence." [10]

In his "Letter to a Hindu," Tolstoy interprets the holy writings of Hinduism to be consistently of a non-violent character. Of one of these scriptures, the Hindu Kural, he says that "The aim of the sinless One lies in not doing evil unto those who have done evil unto him. If a man causes suffering even to those who hate him without any reason, he will ultimately have grief not to be overcome."

Following these passages from the Kural, Tolstoy, referring to attitudes in Russia and Europe, concludes: "The recognition that love represents the highest morality was nowhere denied or contradicted, but this truth was so interwoven with all kinds of falsehoods which distorted it, that finally nothing of it remained but words. It was taught that this highest morality was only applicable to private life—for home use, as it were—but that in public life all forms of violence—such as imprisonment, executions and wars—might be used for the protection of the majority against a minority of evil-doers, though such means were diametrically opposed to any vestige of love."

Tolstoy paints a dark picture of the terrifying perversions into which this highest of moralities has today been transformed, but, strangely enough, he does not call upon those who uphold such a morality to act in a positive and concerted defense of it. In fact, in one of his letters to

Gandhi, Tolstoy went so far as to say that "as soon as resistance is admitted by the side of love, love no longer exists." [12] But it was precisely a positive attitude toward the moral force of love that Gandhi wanted to build; he wanted to evolve and test a strategy which aimed at re-establishing respect and faith in the morality of love. It was essential, moreover, that this be done with the cooperation of those responsible for the distortion. His principles demanded such cooperation and, furthermore, his trust in human nature allowed for its possibility. Co-operation, and inevitably compromise, with authority led, of course, to Gandhi's accepting, for the time being, a number of disagreeable features in the existing institutions. This earned him the alarmed protests of the Tolstoy camp, which rejected any kind of cooperation with any state institution.

In terms of his own political morality, and in contra-distinction to those of Tolstoy, Gandhi was able to lay stress on the disposition of those who did violence, and he rejected, moreover, the idea that the morally negative value of an action increased proportionally to the intensity and extent of the violence employed in it. His attitude toward military organizations was therefore not, as in the case of Tolstoy, one of abhorrence. Gandhi could admire those who fought, in a way they considered to be appropriate, for what they deemed right; if this involved violence then it should be remembered, said Gandhi, that such people are also more likely to be strong enough to employ nonviolent methods than are those who habitually avoid all conflicts and risks. The absence of violence can be due to cowardice; its presence may be due to love.

Gandhi sought, however, to lead the force of love into constructive channels wherever it had gone astray and he was always ready to meet men to try to persuade them to relinquish their trust in violence as a method.

Part Four

GANDHI AND INTERNATIONAL
CONFLICTS OF TODAY

Gandhi after India's political freedom

In an India which in 1947 had gained its political freedom, there was no place for Gandhi to act as a politician;
yet his prevailing influence became even greater than it
had been before. He exerted a powerful influence on
Nehru and the other Congress Party leaders, and his religious influence in Indian culture was immeasurable. One
should be careful, however, not to attribute, either to
Gandhi himself or to his influence, actual political decisions and policies such as those, for instance, that led to
the trouble in Kashmir.

Gandhi still seemed, in 1945-46, to entertain some hopes

that India's politics would be conducted in the spirit of nonviolence. That he was mistaken would not itself be a point of much relevance here, were it not for the widespread misconception that Indian politics are a direct expression of Gandhian ideas.[1] There are some very good reasons for rejecting such a notion.

For instance, when Nehru became Prime Minister in September 1946, the military budget remained as it had been under British rule. To this Gandhi objected: "I have told our people not to depend on the military and the police help. . . . You cannot say it is good in one place and bad in another. The military help will degrade you."[2] Military help spelt "Goodbye to peace." If Indian scientists were required by the state to participate in technical research for war, then, according to Gandhi, they ought to refuse to do so unto death!

Although Gandhi judged the responsibility for bloodshed in Kashmir in 1947 and thereafter in just the way the Indian politicians did, believing that India had the right on her side in her struggle with Pakistan, and hailing the *courage* of the Indian soldiers, he still believed that India should never have resisted Pakistan troops or civilians with physical violence. India, according to Gandhi, might easily have offered Kashmir nonviolent aid, and if the defenders did not surrender, but died at their posts without hatred for their attackers, this would have been a heroic deed, in which India would have played some small part, and which could have lent meaning to the Kashmir dispute for the whole world. But Gandhi admitted that he had no decisive influence on the policies and was but a powerless witness to the violence. When

people did not believe in nonviolence, he could not mobilize nonviolent defense.[3]

Here we are faced with an example of the insuperable
difficulties which leaders of nonviolent action must always encounter. Only when belief in nonviolence is general among the people to whom it is being prescribed
does it make sense to expect nonviolence on any large
scale in any major crisis. During the 1930s Gandhi himself grew increasingly convinced of the fruitlessness, and
even the danger, of calling for nonviolent action in a severe crisis unless he was absolutely certain the spirit and
character of such action would be understood. Furthermore, when the Congress party came into power in 1939,
he saw "decay" setting in, and with it the impossibility of
undertaking civil disobedience, because "though there is
nonviolence enough among the masses, there is not
enough among those who have to organize the masses."
Maybe this could be put more accurately by saying:
though there is enough *potentiality* for nonviolence
among the masses, there is at present not enough among
those who have to organize the masses.

A tragic parallel to Kashmir in 1947 was the Indian
invasion of Goa in 1961. At that later time there was a
corps of "soldiers of nonviolence" two thousand strong,
the Shanti Sena. Narayan, one of its leaders and organiz-
ers, went to Vinoba Bhave when it became clear India
was about to invade Goa, asking Vinoba, the most re-
spected and famous of Gandhi's disciples and head of the
corps, to go to Nehru and propose that the Shanti Sena
be sent to Goa in place of the Army. Vinoba, his interest
now turned exclusively to social and land reform, re-

fused. That such a chance for something less than blood-shed should be missed was a severe blow to the supporters of nonviolence.

Despite, however, Gandhi's clear and consistently negative attitude toward the idea of India having an army, his words do often suggest some support for military power. As early as 1928 he wrote:

If there was a National Government, whilst I should not take any direct part in any war, I can conceive occasions when it would be my duty to vote for the military training of those who wish to take it. For I know that all its members do not believe in non-violence to the extent I do. It is not possible to make a person or a society nonviolent by compulsion.[4]

A respect for an individual's convictions as to how a good cause is to be served best was in Gandhi married to a loyalty to the ideals of democracy. According to those ideals, individuals who do not believe in violence must not forcefully deprive those who do believe in violence of the means of exercising it. The latter must be given the opportunity to train themselves for violence, but should continuously be the target of persuasion of those who want never to use it. That those who believe in nonviolence should try to convert the believers in violence remains a duty of supreme importance.

To many people in the West who read the news from India in 1945-48, Gandhi may well have seemed either to have given up nonviolence in favor of nationalistic militarism, or to have lost all political and moral influence whatsoever. Both impressions are due to failure of communication and understanding. Gandhi was, we should note, an individualist, in so far as he stressed the duty of each individual to follow his conscience and *to help others to follow theirs,* and at the same time a "fallibilist," in so far as he thought that the sense of right and wrong is something that can and must be educated and strengthened, but remains forever prone to error.

It is misleading, without considerable qualifications, therefore, to pin India's failure to find nonviolent solutions on Gandhi's ideas, or to see even in his own apparent condoning of violence a weakening in his ideals.

The political significance of Gandhi's life and teaching

How can Gandhi's teaching contribute at a practical level to the solution of today's international conflicts?

Before answering this question directly, let us examine a misconception prevalent even among those who are favorably inclined toward the use of nonviolent means. A newspaper article in August, 1959, asked "Shouldn't the Tibetans have risen in revolt?" [5] By way of clarification the author wrote: "During a press conference in Mussoorie on 20 June 1959 the Dalai Lama was asked, 'Would passive resistance by your people have given better results than armed revolt?' The Dalai Lama answered, 'Up to the last day I tried to attain a peaceful settlement which did not succeed and so my people turned to armed revolt, being forced to fight for their freedom.' "

Possibly the Dalai Lama was misquoted; but at any rate, he seems to have excluded the possibility of *satyagraha:* the people were "forced to fight for their freedom," says the Dalai Lama. Yes, but a whole people cannot be forced to fight *violently.* Furthermore, if a nonviolent tradition had been established the call to fight would have resulted in *non*violent struggle.

The very expression "passive resistance" seems to indicate that there was from the beginning no real thought of the policy of nonviolence, which is an active measure. The Dalai Lama does not seem to have had any idea of a nonviolent struggle to avert the Chinese Communist domination of Tibet. We should note here, perhaps, that there have been no nonviolent currents in Tibetan politics during this century. Tibet has been isolationist in politics, and isolationism as a philosophy excludes nonviolent policies since such policies necessarily involve the idea of personal contact. Isolationism thus prevented any theoretical basis for Tibetan attempts at nonviolent solutions of conflicts with the Chinese.

Admittedly, however, even if the young Dalai Lama *had* entertained the idea of a nonviolent foreign policy, the chances of his initiating it would have been very small indeed. Gandhi acted as, and was considered, a man of the people; the Dalai Lama acted as, and was considered, a God. He was an isolated individual, shut off from contact with his people.

Consider the sentence "up to the last day, I tried to

attain a peaceful settlement. . . ." This is the standard formulation adopted by governments that have little or no confidence in nonviolence. It omits any mention of the fact that failure of negotiation might indeed force the *satyagrahi* to turn to even stronger means—but means, of course, still within the field of nonviolence. It seems clear that we cannot describe the Tibetan defeat as an unsuccessful attempt to use the means of nonviolence in international politics.

In his book, *My Land and My People,* the Dalai Lama declares himself a believer in nonviolence. "I had and still have unshaken faith in the doctrine of non-violence which [Gandhi] preached and practised." [6] Yet, despite his homage to Gandhi, the Dalai Lama does not seem to have understood that nonviolence at that time could only have been effective if there had been a thorough preparation, not only inside Tibet but also in China. According to Gandhian principles, the *satyagrahi* should proceed to the center of the conflict (see p. 40 above), but the Dalai Lama, though regretting Tibet's isolationism, mentions no attempts at profound contact with the Chinese. In criticizing Tibet's self-exclusion from international affairs, he merely suggests that if Tibet had sought to join the League of Nations or the United Nations, her sovereignty would immediately have been recognized and not "clouded by subtle legal discussions based on ancient treaties . . . ." [7]

We know what terrible events followed the Chinese invasion: widespread execution of the clergy, bombing attacks on Tibetans in no way involved in the struggle, and so on. These are the familiar and senseless brutalities of war. But what they are *not* is evidence of the fact that violent uprising and war comprise the only alternative for a people which an unscrupulous state seeks to obliterate. Gandhi says: "If one believes in violence as the only way to defend high values, one must use it notwithstanding the prospect that it opens up. But if it leads to nothing, the argument for non-violent resistance to physical domination is not thereby destroyed." [8]

The best short answer to the question "Should the Tibetans have rebelled violently, or nonviolently?" seems to be this: Nonviolent methods are only practicable when there are leaders who believe in them. If, therefore, it is true that the Tibetan leaders in 1959 were not convinced of the possibility of nonviolent struggle, the only choice open to them was, as they say, violence or submission.

When answering any questions, such as those above, about the political application of Gandhi's ideas we should, among other things, keep the following factors in view:

1. Gandhi withdrew from regular political life in 1934. Though still influential in politics, he no longer tried to form a practical policy in cooperation with the Nationalist Party. It is entirely misleading, therefore, to judge the policies and actions of the Congress Party as if they were Gandhi's. And even though he was very active during the Second World War, we still have no way of judging how he would have conceived and directed the movement for freedom in the years that followed 1934, had he held any leading political position. If we are to conjecture how a Gandhi-inspired presi-

dent or prime minister would succeed today on the problems that would most concern him, we would be most unwise to look to events in India between 1934 and 1948 for guidance.

2. Gandhianism and anti-militarism are not the same. Nor are *satyagraha* and pacifism as practiced in Europe between the world wars. It is an open question as to whether a movement that favors non-participation in war is or is not consistent with Gandhian teaching. Such a refusal to participate, moreover, can only be a *part* of a political program or action, whether the latter is specifically Gandhian or not. For an action to accord with Gandhi's teaching, it must harmonize with his basic principles and hypotheses, including his teaching on the "constructive program." Anti-militarism, starting with the principle that one should abstain from violence, is, as far as it goes, a negative program, not a constructive one.

3. Disarmament, the development of the United Nations, and solutions to the Cold War, can be, but are not necessarily, in accordance with the Gandhian principles of conflict resolution. These actions in themselves are not the decisive thing; the crucial consideration is whether the framework in which they occur is one of violence or nonviolence, coercion or noncoercion, destructiveness or constructiveness. We must remember that the temporary aggravation of a conflict can well be a part of *satyagraha;* and since Gandhi lent his voice to active intervention in oppression, we could hardly claim his support for a world peace that did not itself countenance such freedom movements as arise through-

Political significance 117

out the world, or at least those that are able to preserve the moral integrity of their purpose. Appeasement and Gandhi's nonviolence are diametrically opposed policies. They have absence of violence in common, but where there is oppression and injustice, Gandhi brings to them conflict, not appeasement or submission.

4. Gandhi has no method to offer to those who struggle for selfish or ethically neutral ends. Appeals to support "the West" lack any Gandhian force unless devoid of the usual ingredients of power politics. But how many make, or interpret, such appeals in this rather than in, for example, the NATOesque way, which sees them as some kind of worthy extension of ordinary power politics in the noble defense of "truth and humanity"?

Points Two and Three have a special importance, and if they are neglected, one is prevented from seeing the central and original conviction of Gandhi's teaching: that truth, love, nonviolent standards of conduct, trust in nonviolent methods, and the duty to carry out constructive programs all work for the resolution of conflicts.

If disarmament is not universal but only regional, and if disarmed nations neglect to mobilize strong forces of nonviolence for the pursuit and protection of their valid and just international goals, then these countries will be just as weak as they were before, possibly even weaker if they have disarmed themselves out of fear, resignation, defeatism, or out of scepticism about the value of military protectiveness, combined with doubt or ignorance about the possibilities of nonviolent offense.

One accepted move, for example, a move supposedly

"in the right direction" toward ending the Cold War, is for the opponents to make mutual promises that they will not try to influence conditions in other countries. But, of course, such a bargain is completely in violation of the spirit of Gandhian political action. Part of the population in Soviet Russia and Eastern Europe have been led to believe that there are people in "the West" who live in such terrible conditions that it is the duty of Russian and Eastern European citizens to come to their aid. Corresponding ideas can be found in "the West" concerning people in "the East." But if we are to adopt Gandhian principles, we cannot view these unusual pleas lightly; for according to Gandhi, all life, in the last analysis, is one, and therefore cruelty to one is cruelty to all. The borders between countries mean nothing. So long, therefore, as we retain such beliefs about the conditions of such people's lives, it follows that we must try to exert some kind of beneficial influence on their behalf. That is, we *must* try to interfere, and this may well create considerable friction. Every step, of course, must first be taken to become acquainted with all of the relevant facts about a country and we must be sure that our efforts will indeed assist those they are designed to help. Good intentions are not enough. Furthermore, if oppression and violence are practiced in our own country, then our efforts at helping others may become mere parody. There are, in sum, many conditions which must be fulfilled in order to justify large-scale interference in other countries.

This brings us to the fourth point. Gandhi could never have conceived *satyagraha* as an effective means of maintaining international domination, or even of balancing power, nor of protecting, in any way, national interests when such interests oppose those of others or enable a nation, for example, to secure economic hegemony over underdeveloped countries. Since these points are so vital, they bear some elaboration.

Can nonviolent defense replace military defense?

Nowadays, just as before, military defense is an instrument in the hands of individual nations. The aims of defense are, of course, primarily national—the safeguarding of a nation's interests as a whole. The word "defense," however, when we use it in connection with the kind of military power we have today, can be merely a "pious euphemism," as it has been called. We talk of "defense power" as though it were exclusively a tool to prevent the aggression of foreign states. If only this were so, it might indeed make good sense to say that the military factor could be replaced by a nonviolent one. However, no one acquainted with foreign affairs could come to assign to "defense power" so meager a role, or think of it with such innocence.

Any application of Gandhian principles to present-day

international conflicts presupposes that, instead of a straightforward political *definition* of ends, one should make a critical *evaluation* of them, and that in so doing all ends that are ethically untenable or ethically irrelevant be put aside. According to Gandhi's teaching, particularly as illustrated in the initial phases of his campaigns, the motivation and the definition of an aim must be clear and unequivocal, and all the relevant circumstances thoroughly investigated before the struggle is finally set in motion.

Military enterprises, as we know, can succeed in their aims regardless of the motives of those who undertake them. With nonviolent struggles, however, it is quite the reverse. For, according to Gandhi, the results of any contest, whatever qualities of courage, discipline, and morale the antagonists might display in it, acquire their justification solely by virtue of a prior process of purification. Applied internationally, this means that Britain or the United States, say, can only properly be said to conduct their foreign policies according to genuine nonviolent principles if (1) their populations are well-informed about the conditions in those countries to which its foreign policy is directed, (2) the populations in those other countries are willing and able to judge the advances made toward them as ones based on moral grounds rather than as acts of expediency, and (3) can base their reaction to them on the same standards.

When we consider how limited the knowledge is of the countries that are seriously affected by foreign policies, the contrast between the contemporary situation and that of Gandhi's followers in India and South Africa becomes

acutely apparent. Certainly Gandhi's politics had reper-
cussions in Britain: the workers in the British textile industry are a case in point; but through personal contacts
and a steady exchange of information, a certain level of
communication between the various antagonists could
always be maintained. It is clear that such a situation is
the exception rather than the rule, and that this is so is,
no doubt, as often the intention as well as the result of
the policies meted out by the nations to their "opposite"
numbers.

It is vitally important here, obviously, to see what kind
of national policy could fruitfully be applied to the present international situation and to see, at the same time, if
it could be a genuinely Gandhian one. We shall conclude
by a presentation of a five-point strategy which is intended
to fulfill these two requirements.

Five programs for building
nonviolent power

The programs suggested here contain policies designed to
promote strength and national "power" without being
destructive or coercive, and without leading to any increase in violence. It is important to note that "power,"
here and in the ensuing discussion of nonviolent strate-

gies, must be defined in terms of *influence,* and not in terms of military might or war-potential. Power in this sense is something that both militarists and anti-militarists would be glad to have, albeit for different reasons.

If military strength were today greatly reduced, in the absence of any other significant changes, many people would justifiably feel even less secure from danger than they do already; their passive state of despair and fatalism would be reinforced. If, that is, the only means a person believes to be effective in solving a problem are no longer available to him, he has every reason to feel frustrated and deprived. Clearly then, a decrease in military strength must be preceded by the cultivation of a greater confidence in alternative means of defense. Current criticism of foreign policies is apparently based, however, far more on doubts about the value of armaments than on confidence in non-military ways of defense. The result is that the struggle for disarmament has come either to be associated with the rather utopian belief that no organized defense of freedom is necessary once there is disarmament, or with the feeling that there is no meaningful way at all to counteract tendencies toward dictatorship. If we recall the principle which said that we should make a constructive program part of our campaign and, as far as possible, give to all phases of any struggle a constructive character, one reason at least thus clearly suggests itself for the relative ineffectiveness of many disarmament efforts.

The following programs are motivated by the desire to construct a non-coercive foreign policy and a non-military defense policy, both of which would be determined

Five programs 123

by the political and military realities of our day. But those realities being what they are, this strategy obviously cannot ask either for immediate disarmament, or for disarmament alone.

1. *Clarification of national commitments.* The prime need of any nation is a program for the clarification of its national ideals, commitments, and goals. There are two reasons why this is the most necessary step for non-military defense, but even apart from these, it should be recognized that such a program is good for the nation no matter what form of defense it ultimately employs.

The main purpose of such a program would be, simply enough, to get citizens to understand what it is they are willing to defend. The morale and the efficiency of a people engaged in defending "a way of life" very much depends upon the extent to which they realize what that "way of life" is. A program, therefore, of working toward the most widespread understanding of the ideas, ideals and moral convictions which are associated with freedom and not with violence, is of tremendous importance.

But the program is also of importance in so far as the definition of group goals in a struggle is something which must come before the struggle itself. According to Gandhi, the clearer you make yourself about the essential points in your cause and struggle, the less likely you are to take a violent attitude. Furthermore, the better your opponent understands your conduct and your case, the less likely he is to use violent means.

The step-by-step clarification of goals is an immense task. Discussion groups, debates, articles, books, etc., must be enlisted in support of this self-examination—a self-examination which must be carried out with the broadest cross-cultural knowledge of all those traits common to different ways of life. The task is, in a sense, an "ideological" one, but in quite a different sense from those detailed, articulated systems of conduct and goals which seek to compel compliance and to produce total conversion.

The program must consist very largely of increasing the involvement of those vast numbers of people who hardly trouble themselves at all to think out or define those things for which they stand, or even would like to stand. Vital in this respect would be the encouragement of direct man-to-man discussions between people from different countries. It would mean lifting travel restrictions, facilitating travel in other ways, and encouraging those encounters which are most conducive to the growth of cross-loyalties; and this, among other things, would require us to meet foreigners as individuals, not as symbols of their countries.

In the Soviet Union, the United States, and in many other powerful nations, contacts of the kind which multiply loyalties and clarify national purposes have often been avoided, or never have been encouraged because of a fear that arguments directed against the dominant political system might prove too winning, and would then result in "converts," persons cooperating with potential "enemies." It is, of course, impossible to justify such an attitude unless one is happy to leave political education to demagogic indoctrination or to the black and white simplifications of school text-books. Nonviolent defense implies, after all, an intimate contact with "the enemy" and therefore the kind of education needed to discuss historical, political, and ideological matters with him.

Paradoxically, we could say that the more we render our defenses vulnerable to blows from the outside world, the less vulnerable our society becomes. Failing any fruitful self-examination in the light of criticism from "foreigners," however, the result of future emergencies and contact with "the enemy" might well be that he will gain more converts than would have been the case had the average citizen been treated as a free and responsible person, a person with the full right to objective information.

2. *International service.* As a means of defense, international service (like other non-military means of defense) should be undertaken primarily for its own sake. International service aims at relieving human poverty, suffering, and threats to personal indignity and integrity. If *participants* in international service serve only because their doing so will assist a defense effort, this inevitably reduces or destroys many of the intrinsic values of the service, as well, ultimately, as its contribution to defense. For policymakers it is important, however, to recognize the relation between international service and the defense problem:

Firstly, international service can remove important *causes* of conflicts and wars by contributing to the establishment of conditions favorable to conflicts without violence.

Secondly, international service can strengthen, can encourage, peaceful "man-to-man" interaction between potential "enemies," and thereby contribute to the development of personal loyalties between individuals of various countries, factions, and races. Even if sponsored by national governments, the service should move from individual to individual, rather than from nation to nation. The idea, let us recall, that one's primary affiliations are with one's country is, according to Gandhi, a false and hazardous one. Personal contacts are, to put it briefly, superior to national projects.

Thirdly, international service, with no political "strings" attached, can contribute to the development in other countries of a positive attitude toward its sponsors. This, of course, reduces the chance of aggression against them. A potential "enemy," that is, would see from our self-sacrifice that our intentions were not aggressive—something which he would never be able to see if we were to remain fundamentally isolationist. Furthermore, in the event of a crisis, any country's plight would receive far greater attention, publicity, sympathy and aid once it had demonstrated that it was consistently dedicated to such international goals as constructive international service and non-military aid. For small countries, like Switzerland and the Scandinavian ones, this fact is of great importance and is, in short, what would prevent them from being swallowed or annihilated in a clash between great powers.

Fourthly, participation in international service can offer valuable training in sustaining a high morale under adverse conditions, and in learning that discipline which is part of working and suffering for a great common cause. The ability of people to practice such cooperation in times of crisis in *their own country* will thereafter be decidedly enhanced. It will minimize the danger of wanton violence and of fifth columnism, and will provide the leadership with a people capable of individual initiative under the most extreme conditions.

Finally, those who directly receive help from a country will behave more sympathetically toward that country in the case of a later conflict. (Thus the number of starving Austrian children who in 1918 were invited to Norway behaved magnificently and avoided violence when they returned to Norway as soldiers and administrators during the 1940-45 Nazi occupation.)

A program of large-scale international service would call for great private and governmental expenditure. Under present conditions, the cost would have to be largely in addition to the military budget, which would mean an increase in taxes. For the rich countries of the West, such added costs would not lead to bankruptcy, and for others much could be done simply by reshaping their economies and their educational institutions.

3. *Improving our own society.* A non-military defense program would give us a society far more worth defending. "Housecleaning" by the whole society is required by the very idea of nonviolent defense; a society must not only deserve to be defended, it must realize that any of its institutions, if based on ideas of an "enemy," or of "bad people" rather than bad deeds, are simply inconsistent with nonviolence.

Certain aspects of decentralization must be encouraged, whether or not such decentralization is desirable in all of its respects. Individual citizens will have to learn to make decisions for themselves in small groups, and to become less and less dependent upon the government or the leaders of large organizations. Those institutions in our society which do train the individual to make responsible decisions in time of crisis must be strengthened lest demoralization, inertia, and anarchy ensue should the state apparatus be suddenly captured by an invader or destroyed in atomic warfare.

4. *Non-military resistance.* Unfortunately, the customary way in which *military* defeat and *total* defeat are thought to be the same prevents any discussion of the problems of occupation at the government level; such discussion is considered there to be "defeatist" or deficient in "defense-mindedness." In fact, however, the reverse is far nearer the truth, for by thinking military and total defeat to be the same, some people neglect a vitally important sector of defense, and thus reveal *themselves* to be seriously lacking in defense-mindedness.

An invading power should be met, that is, with whatever form of nonviolent resistance can best be adapted to the case, whenever that power attempts to extend its domain by *forcing inhabitants to violate their basic principles.* Even, for example, if a country's major institutions were all taken over or demolished, and all recognized leaders executed, and even in the event of extensive deportations, nonviolence might be the only means to safeguard the rights, dignity and integrity of the individuals who survive.

5. *Research.* Non-military means of defense have in the last decade been studied, in a preliminary sort of way,

from the strategical point of view. But nothing comparable to the extent or quality of military research has developed in this new-born area. A foreign policy devoid of threats of mass violence has as yet been thought unworthy of implementation. However, the creation of numerous peace research institutes, in part sponsored by national governments, suggests at least a growing interest in this area, as did the first representative international study conference of civilian defense at Oxford in 1964.

In conclusion, it might not be out of place in this very brief study to say once again that every attempt in the field of foreign affairs to identify a specifically Gandhian course cannot avoid being highly subjective. This follows from the nature of the highly complex considerations involved in any matter of foreign affairs. There can be no rule-books of Gandhian policy. There are no easy Gandhian formulae. This, however, does not necessarily reduce the value of Gandhi's teaching in the contemporary political situation. After all, the indication of direction that a compass-needle gives is of some value in itself, even if it takes no consideration of the terrain through which we must pass.

NOTES

1. Those who want a solid basis for a critical evaluation of Gandhi's moral attainments are referred to Louis Fischer's biography for information on the young Gandhi, and to N. K. Bose's *Studies in Gandhism* for his later years.

2. Compare the two opposing trends in crowd psychology led, respectively, by Gustave Le Bon and F. H. Allport. Le Bon proposed, in *Psychologie des Foules* (orig. 1895) Paris: Alcan, 1937 ed., Engl. trans. *Crowds,* Viking, 1960, that a crowd's conduct and psychology differ essentially from the

individual's. Among his pupils, W. D. Scott, in *The Psychology of Public Speaking,* London and New York: Pearson Bros. 1907, has stressed that a crowd has a high emotional level and lacks the feeling of responsibility; and E. O. Martin, in *The Behavior of Crowds,* New York: Harper, 1920, described the psychopathic character a crowd can display in giving vent to its repressed impulses to aggression and sadism. In opposition to Le Bon's school, Allport, in his *Social Psychology,* New York: Houghton, 1924, proposed that individuals in crowds acted as though they were alone, "only more so" (p. 295). Allport does not accept Le Bon's claim that a "crowd mind," with its own characteristics, is formed.

3. M. K. Gandhi, *An Autobiography or the Story of My Experiments with Truth,* Ahmedabad: Navajivan Publishing House, 1927, 1956 ed., p. 214.

4. For an account of this episode, see D. G. Tendulkar, *Mahatma,* Vol. 7, Jhaveri and Tendulkar, Bombay, 1953, pp. 146-8. Also M. K. Gandhi, *Satyagraha in South Africa,* Ahmedabad: Navajivan Publishing House, 1950, p. 325, and G. N. Dhawan, *The Political Philosophy of Mahatma Gandhi,* Bombay: Popular Book Depot, 1946, Ahmedabad: Navajivan Publishing House, 1951, p. 201 (1946 ed.).

5. It is perhaps worthwhile to recall in passing the debate on "mass man" in social psychology. Gustave Le Bon's *Psychologie des Foules* (1895) has contributed a great deal to our conception of the deterioration of man *en masse.* William McDougall and later psychologists have done something to correct this view, Le Bon's account being shown to apply only to spontaneously formed groups that have no firm inner organization. McDougall grants that groups may act recklessly, and in a primitive and uncontrolled way, but that there are conditions under which they may also behave rationally and display considerable morale and unselfishness. See, W. McDougall, *The Group Mind.* Cambridge: Cambridge Univ. Press, 1920.

6. This, of course, is not to say that the amount of energy which an individual is actually able to put into realiz-

ing a moral principle is a direct measure of moral worth. A man of quite ordinary ability, placed in an environment which restricts his development, perhaps wasted by disease and with a number of undeserved disabilities, is not thereby prevented from reaching as great a level of *moral* excellence as a man who is brilliantly endowed in every way; but very likely, of course, the former individual will be far less effectual, and the actual energy of his attempt to comply with a moral principle may never be sufficient to give rise to any significant result (characters in Grahame Greene's novels could be mentioned here). If we are not to confuse moral worth with greatness, with what Kierkegaard called "the world-historical," the weak must be put on an equal footing with the mighty.

7. John Ruskin, "The Roots of Honour," *Unto this Last,* Four Essays on the First Principles of Political Economy, 6th ed., Orpington 1888, pp. 3-4.

8. Let us say that if the degree of purity was arranged along an x-axis and the effect along a y-axis the function we are referring to can be graphically represented as a curve according to which every increase in x would become more nearly perpendicular along the y-axis.

PART TWO
The Content of Gandhi's Political Ethics

1. The word "hypothesis" is not meant in this context to suggest uncertainty. The main consideration is that hypotheses be distinct from principles, that is, be descriptive and confirmable.

2. Indeed, this would seem to be a feature typical of many ethical doctrines: that, though they are often formulated in quite simple language, they function less as straightforward accounts of reality than as keys to the discovery of new sets of connections in things, the sum total of which may not at all be adequately described in terms of the original statements.

3. *"Ahimsa"* I have translated as "nonviolence" (without a hyphen). The much broader concept of "absence of physical violence to persons" I have called "non-violence." Accordingly, I have distinguished "nonviolent defense" and "non-violent" or "non-military" defense. The new term "civilian defense" seems to acquire a rather broad significance between the narrow "nonviolent defense" and the very broad "non-violent" or "non-military defense." I would prefer a rather narrow connotation, one excluding coercion and tricks of psychological warfare. A broader connotation, however, will make it more palatable to most of those people who are today contributing to our ideas in the field of national defense—including some military strategists.

4. One of its most concentrated expressions as well as concrete contributions is to be found in Johan Galtung's book *Forsvar uten militærvesen. Et pasifistisk grunnsyn* (Defense Without Military Weapons. A Pacifist View), publ. by Folkereisning mot Krig. n.d.

5. *Young India* (henceforth, Y.I.), 31 Dec. '31, in Prabhu, R. K. and Rao, U. R., *The Mind of Mahatma Gandhi*, Oxford University Press, 1946, p. 29.

6. *Harijan* (henceforth, H.), 23 June '46, in Gandhi, M. K., *Non-violence in Peace and War*, Vol. 2, Ahmedabad: Navajivan Publishing House, 1949, pp. 104-5.

7. Y.I. 13 April '24, in Prabhu and Rao, *op. cit.*, p. 158.

8. Gandhi, M. K., *Yeravda Mandir*, Ahmedabad: Navajivan Publishing House, 2nd ed., 1935; in Bose, N. K. *Selections from Gandhi*, Ahmedabad: Navajivan Publishing House, 1957, p. 257.

9. Gandhi, M. K., *An Autobiography, or the Story of My Experiments with Truth*, 1956 ed., pp. xiii-xiv.

10. Prabhu and Rao, *op. cit.*, p. 179 (from an address delivered 16 Feb. 1916).

11. H., 6 July '40, in M. K. Gandhi, *Non-violence in Peace and War*, Vol. 1, pp. 281-2.

12. H., 9 June '46, in Gandhi, M. K., *Non-violence in Peace and War*, Vol. 2, p. 69.

13. Y.I., 26 Dec. '24, in Prabhu and Rao, *op. cit.*, p. 196.

14. *Non-violence in Peace and War*, Vol. 1, p. 199.

15. Y.I., 17 July '24, in Prabhu and Rao, *op. cit.*, p. 196.

16. From the *Amrit Bazar Patrika* in N. K. Bose, *op. cit.*, p. 36.

17. Y.I., 20 May '26, in M. K. Gandhi, *For Pacifists*, Ahmedabad: Navajivan Publishing House, 1949, p. 48.

18. *Autobiography* . . . , (1956 ed.) p. 504.

19. H., 24 Dec. '38 in Prabhu and Rao, *op. cit.*, p. 81.

20. H., 4 March '39 in M. K. Gandhi, *To Students*, Ahmedabad, Navajivan Publishing House, 1953, p. 63.

21. As in M. Biardeau's article, "Gandhi, histoire et légende," *Esprit*, 1954, p. 191.

22. D. G. Tendulkar, *Mahatma*, Vol. 2, Bombay 1951, pp. 23-24.

23. Pyarelal, *Mahatma Gandhi, The Last Phase*, Vol. 1, Ahmedabad: Navajivan Publishing House, 1956, p. 572.

24. Romain Rolland, *Inde, Journal 1915-1943*, Paris: Editions Vineta, 1951, p. 38.

25. D. G. Tendulkar, *loc. cit.*

26. This is shown, among other things, by the fact that after the liberation, much of Gandhi's reform work came to a standstill: "In 1948, a few months after Gandhi's death, those who had been associated with the old man's village work and who had resisted the lure of high office met in Sevagram to form a new Society. Already independence had disillusioned them with politics. Such success as Gandhi's social programme—cottage industries, decentralisation and non-violence—had obtained seemed to have been due to its political significance as an attempt to undermine British

power rather than to any real acceptance of its message on the part of the politicians." H. Tennyson, *Saint on the March, The Story of Vinoba,* London: Gollancz, 1956, p. 44.

27. This is best done in a number of steps, so that contribution to the self-realization of all becomes a self-sufficient end, and constant help becomes the only adequate means.

28. P. Kropotkin, *Mutual Aid, A Factor of Evolution,* Heinemann, London 1902, popular edition 1915.

29. Gopi Nath Dhawan, *The Political Philosophy of Mahatma Gandhi,* 1946 ed., pp. 4-5.

30. Gandhi went so far as to say that if we showed confidence to snakes and scorpions, they shouldn't sting or bite. We must acknowledge this to be a rather far-reaching generalization from the hypothesis in question. Scorpions and snakes were allowed to crawl freely in and out of the rooms. Miss Madeleine Slade, who was a member of one of the *ashrams,* recounts that all the people did to protect themselves was to move with sliding steps so that the animals were moved to the side instead of trampled on. In Gandhi's animal psychology, it is, however, conceded that snakes and scorpions cannot altogether distinguish between carelessness and hostility. They may well attack someone who tramples on them quite by mistake. Miss Slade did close doors with some caution, for she knew that there might have been large snakes sleeping on the other side of them. Nobody likes to be awakened by being hit by a door.

31. H., 24 June 1939.

32. M. K. Gandhi, *Yeravda Mandir,* in Bose, N. K., *op. cit.,* p. 257.

33. Gora (G. Ramachandra Rao), *An Atheist with Gandhi,* Ahmedabad: Navajivan Publishing House, 1951, p. 27.

34. *Ibid.,* pp. 30-31.

35. *Ibid.,* p. 32.

36. *Ibid.,* p. 35.

37. *Ibid.*, p. 38.

38. I mention this to show how dubious is that opinion, coming from such important critics as Otto Wolff and others, that Gandhi's regime did not allow the individual to develop his personal abilities.

39. *Ibid.*, p. 48.

40. *Ibid.*, p. 56.

41. *Ibid.*, p. 51.

42. *Ibid.*, p. 59.

43. *Ibid.*, p. 44.

44. H., 29 April '39, in Dhawan, *op. cit.*, p. 125.

45. Published in Rolland Romain, *Inde, Journal 1915-1943,* p. 32.

46. M. K. Gandhi, *Satyagraha in South Africa,* p. 115.

47. *Ibid.*, pp. 109-10.

48. Y.I., 20 Oct. '27, in Prabhu and Rao, *op. cit.*, p. 75.

49. See, for example, Johan Galtung and Arne Naess, *Gandhis politiske etikk,* Oslo: J. G. Tanum, 1965, Norwegian, pp. 225-44; Diwakar, R. R. *Satyagraha: Its Technique and History,* Bombay: pp. 48-49.

50. The expression "civil disobedience" was first used by the American writer and sage, Henry David Thoreau, in 1841. He wrote his essay "On the Duty of Civil Disobedience" after he had been jailed for failure to pay his poll-tax to a state which supported slavery. Gandhi, who knew the essay, interpreted "civil disobedience" in the sense of "peaceful," "polite," "non-violent disobedience," (*cf.* M. K. Gandhi, *Satyagraha,* Ahmedabad: Navajivan Publishing House, 1951, pp. 3, 172 and 306) i.e., as the opposite of "militant" rather than of "military" disobedience.

51. Galtung and Naess (*Gandhis politiske etikk*) mention a kind of action that would be classified as "ultima-

tum." For instance, someone makes a certain request of his opponent and says, for example, that if such and such reforms are not made or such and such negotiations conducted, then certain action will be taken. I think this category should be omitted. If an ultimatum is to be understood as a threat, it is incompatible with Gandhian principles. On the other hand, when an action is contemplated, something that might appear to be an ultimatum might be necessary in order to fulfill the requirement that all plans be laid before one's opponents. If the motive is in accordance with the principles, it will be mainly a motive to make clear to the opposition what those plans are. The motive should not be: if we now make such and such threats, we will see whether or not the opposition is in a condition to give way to them.

52. Karl Jaspers, *Die Atombombe und die Zukunft des Menschen,* R. Piper and Co., Munich 1958, English translation *The Future of Mankind,* Chicago: University of Chicago Press, 1961, pp. 63f.

53. In *Non-violence in Peace and War,* Vol. 2, p. 362. Paullin and Bondurant adhere to the definition of "coercion" as "the use of either physical or intangible force to compel action contrary to the will or reasoned judgment of the individual or group subjected to such force." This is indeed a good formulation of one of the connotations of "coercion." But how does nonviolence or even *satyagraha involve* coercion in this sense? Bondurant (*Conquest of Violence,* Princeton: Princeton University Press, 1958, p. 9) claims that, e.g., boycott involves coercion. If Indians do not buy British clothing and the merchant has to send a great many shirts back to England, is the merchant in that case compelled to do something contrary to his will or reasoned judgment? Even if he is blind and deaf to the positive side of the boycott, he is not compelled to act *unreasonably.* Heavy rain or strong arguments may compel me to stay at home, and stay at home I will, with good reason and not at all contrary to my will.

To say that *satyagraha* is something which *involves* coercion seems to me to go too far in accommodating possibly undesirable or non-intended consequences to an action. Given a *satyagraha* campaign, it is an empirical question whether it actually coerces anybody and how much it does so. The matter is *mainly* one of terminology, one might say, but it is one not without some importance when distinguishing Gandhi's *intended* approach from the ordinary non-military approaches which possess comparatively modest ethical requirements.

54. Jaspers, *op. cit.*, p. 63. The widespread use of the term "non-violent coercion" has lent credence to this misleading opinion of Jaspers. The use of the terms "coercion" and "compulsion" shows some differences. In certain senses, Gandhi found it justifiable for a *satyagraha* leader to coerce or compel, in other senses he did not. I think it leads to less misunderstanding to use the terms in such a way that Gandhi is shown to be *against* coercion and compulsion. In the list of usages described by H. Ofstad (see following) use (b) is such a use, (a) and (c) are not.

"A person who steals because he is a kleptomaniac may be said to be the victim of internal compulsion. To say so does not prejudge the question whether he had it in his power to resist the compulsion.

"In order to clarify somewhat the talk about inner compulsion, it seems convenient to distinguish between the five following analyses:

"(a) P's decision was an outcome of a conflict which was not solved through the process of decision. When the decision-making started, P wanted both x and y, but could not have both. And when the decision had been made in favor of x, P still desired y.

"This is a broad sense of the term. Most of our decisions are probably compelled in this sense. In most of our decisions we have to sacrifice certain goods in order to realize some others.

"(b) P's decision was determined by tensions, drives, needs, motives, etc., with which he did not identify himself. According to this line of analysis, we do not talk about 'inner compulsion' if the tension-system representing the self won the victory, even if the tension was at a very high level. But sometimes (c) we talk about decisions as being compelled if the tension was high, even if the person identified himself with the motivation in question. This distinction should be kept in mind, since a decision which is compelled in one of these senses may not be so in relation to the other." (*An Inquiry into the Freedom of Decision,* Oslo: Norwegian University Press, London: Allen and Unwin, New York: Humanities Press, 1961, p. 40)

55. Jaspers, *op. cit.* Eng. trans., p. 39.

PART THREE
Gandhi's Political Morality Compared to the Political Moralities of Luther, Hobbes, Nietzsche, and Tolstoy

1. Anders Nygren, "Luther och staten," *Svensk Tidskrift,* Uppsala, 1942, pp. 99, 101.

2. Y. I., 9 May '29, in M. K. Gandhi, *For Pacifists,* p. 56.

3. Johan Hygen, *Albert Schweitzers tanker om kulturen,* Oslo: Forlaget Land og Kirke, 1954, pp. 58-59. Cf. Schweitzer's *Kultur und Ethik,* C. H. Beck 1960, p. 59.

4. S. King-Hall, *Defence in the Nuclear Age,* London: Gollancz, 1958, p. 22. It is worthwhile noting that the term "war" (*bellum*) is used by Hobbes in a very wide sense, quite close to the old Germanic word "werre" which Commander Sir Stephen King-Hall is now trying to revive.

5. "Ara der deutschen Verdummung," *Werke* (Grossoctavausgabe), XIII, p. 350. In Crane Brinton, *Nietzsche,* Cambridge, Mass., Harvard University Press, 1941.

6. Sources for studying Nietzsche's life often lend themselves to interpretation by means of individual rather than social psychology. This seems evident at least in the cases of the biographical studies by Elizabeth Förster-Nietzsche, A. Ahlberg, Carl Roos, and H. A. Reyburn. The difference in

scope and quality of the critical literature in the cases of Nietzsche and Gandhi is enormous. Compared with Gandhi, Nietzsche is almost unknown to us.

7. M. P. Nicolas, *From Nietzsche Down to Hitler*, trans. from French, London, 1938, p. 125.

8. For literature on Nietzsche's reputation and influence, see Brinton, *op, cit.* pp. 256ff.

9. For a detailed, non-literal interpretation of Zarathustra, see August Messer, *Erläuterunges zu Nietzsche's Zarathustra*, Stuttgart, 1922.

10. Romain Rolland. *Mahatma Gandhi:* the man who became one with the universal being, New York and London, Century Co., 1924, p. 147.

11. Tolstoy's letter, with an introduction by Gandhi, appears in print in Kalida Nag, *Tolstoy and Gandhi*, Patna: Pustak Bhandar, 1950, p. 86.

12. In Nag, *op. cit.* p. 72.

PART FOUR
*Gandhi and
International Conflicts of Today*

1. An interesting article by James Bristol which shows an intention on India's part to conduct a military policy in the spirit of Gandhi is to be found in *Peace News,* Oct. 1959. Concerning those people who stood by Gandhi when he was still alive, Bristol says, among other things, "What alarmed me (and I know of other Western pacifists who have also become alarmed) was the fact that far too few of these men display that same vigorous criticism of their own country's arms preparation that they give eloquent expression to when it's a matter of the great powers arming themselves."

2. D. G. Tendulkar, *Mahatma*, Vol. 7, 1945-47, p. 334.

3. For corroboration of this, see, for example, Pyarelal, *Mahatma Gandhi. The Last Phase,* Vol. 2, 1958, pp. 502ff. The relationship between Gandhi and India's policies, and particularly the contrast, is one of the topics discussed in Gene Sharp's *Gandhi Faces the Storm* (Unpublished).

4. Y. I., 13 Sept. '28. Prabhu and Rao, *op. cit.* p. 65.

5. Translated from Rolf Thue, "Gandhi-laere og Tibet-laerdom," *Aftenposten* (Oslo), 28 August 1959, afternoon edition. I mean here only to illustrate the difference between violent and nonviolent strategy. Whether the Dalai Lama actually did use the words he is quoted as using and whether conditions in Tibet in 1959 were as described, I am not at all competent to judge.

6. *My Land and My People,* London: Weidenfeld and Nicolson, 1962, pp. 131-62.

7. *Ibid.,* p. 79.

8. D. G. Tendulkar, *Mahatma,* Vol. 8, p. 136.

Selected bibliography of books in English
With an emphasis on more recent publications

Buchan, Alastair, "Forward" in *Civilian Defence*, published by *Peace News*, London 1964. An appraisal of civilian defense by the Director of the Institute for Strategic Studies, London.

Bondurant, Joan V. *Conquest of Violence. The Gandhian Philosophy of Conflict*, Princeton, New Jersey: Princeton University Press, 1958. This is the first book by a social scientist from the Western hemisphere to deal with the significance of Gandhi and *satyagraha* for problems within political theory and practice in the West. The author stresses the significance of *satyagraha* as "a theoretical key to the problems of social and political conflict."

Bose, Nirmal Kumar (editor). *Selections from Gandhi,* Ahmedabad: Navajivan Publishing House, Second (enlarged) Edition, 1957. A good collection of Gandhi's thoughts on religious, social, economic and political questions.

Bose, Nirmal Kumar. *Studies in Gandhism,* 2nd ed., Calcutta: Indian Associated Publishing Co., 1947. Essays on Gandhi's thinking in economics and politics, including his sociopolitical action method.

Civilian Defense, a *Peace News* pamphlet, London, 1964. Contains articles by J. D. Frank, Arne Naess, A. Roberts, G. Sharp and a foreword by the Hon. Alastair Buchan.

Desai, Mahadev. *The Gospel of Selfless Action or The Gita According to Gandhi,* Ahmedabad: Navajivan Publishing House, (1946) 1951. English translation, by Gandhi's secretary, of a commentary on Gandhi's translation, in Gujarati, of the Bhagavad Gita. Gandhi's translation and interpretation stress the moral value of disengaged action, such as he considered so important in *satyagraha.* Casts much light on Gandhi's attitude toward Hinduism as a religion.

Dhawan, Gopi Nath. *The Political Philosophy of Mahatma Gandhi,* revised ed., Ahmedabad: Navajivan Publishing House, 1957. One of the first works by a social scientist about the significance of Gandhi's method. A useful book, in spite of the author's frequently uncritical attitude.

Diwakar, Ranganath R. *Satyagraha: Its Technique and History,* with a foreword by Dr. Rajendra Prasad, Bombay: Hind Kitabs Publishers, 1946. A short survey of the nature, methods, and history of *satyagraha* by an admirer of Gandhi.

Duncan, Ronald. *Selected Writings of Mahatma Gandhi,* London: Faber and Faber, Boston: Beacon Press, 1951. With a twenty-page foreword by Duncan: a collection of choice quotations and aphorisms.

Fischer, Louis. *The Life of Mahatma Gandhi,* New York:

Harper & Bros., 1950. One of the best documented and best written biographies.

Galtung, Johan. "Pacifism from a Sociological Point of View," *Journal of Conflict Resolution,* Vol. III, no. 1 (March 1959), pp. 67-84. Account and definition of "pacifism" with the help of sociological concepts and theories.

Gandhi, M. K. *All Men are Brothers. Life and Thoughts of Mahatma Gandhi as Told in his own Words,* with an introduction by S. Radhakrishnan. Paris: UNESCO, 1958. One of the best collections of extracts from Gandhi's writings. Deals with a wide range of religious, social, political, and economic questions.

Gandhi, M. K. *An Autobiography or the Story of My Experiments with Truth.* Ahmedabad: Navajivan Publishing House, (1927) 1956. Gandhi's autobiography up to 1921, with stress on his religious and political development. Of fundamental importance to the study of Gandhi's understanding of his own significance.

Gandhi, M. K. *Christian Missions. Their Place in India,* Ahmedabad: Navajivan Publishing House, (1941) 1957. A collection of Gandhi's articles on this topic.

Gandhi, M. K. *Non-violence in Peace and War,* Ahmedabad: Navajivan Publishing House, Vol. I (1942) 1948, Vol. II, 1949. A very good collection of Gandhi's articles and sayings from 1920 to 1948 on the relation of non-violent methods to social and political questions, on both a national and an international level. The first volume particularly important. Indispensable for any study of Gandhi.

Gandhi, M. K. *Satyagraha,* Ahmedabad: Navajivan Publishing House, 1951. A collection of Gandhi's articles and sayings on the character and use of his sociopolitical action method.

Gandhi, M. K. *Satyagraha in South Africa,* Ahmedabad: Navajivan Publishing House (1928), 1950. Gandhi's own account of the origin and development of the *satyagraha* campaign in the Indian minority in South Africa.

Harijan, weekly newspaper, started 11 February 1933, published in Poona and later in Ahmedabad. Edited by M. K. Gandhi, occasionally by others. The period 16 August 1942 to February 1946 saw no publication of the paper. *Harijan* (see also *Young India*) is a basic source for Gandhi's writings from 1933 until his death on January 30th, 1948.

Janis, Irving L. and Daniel Katz. "The Reaction of Intergroup Hostility. Research Problems and Hypotheses," *Journal of Conflict Resolution,* Vol. III, no. 1 (March 1959), pp. 85-100. Examination of "the new and promising areas of research in social psychology which are indicated by different ethical propositions relating to methods for reducing hostility between groups and mutual advancement concluding in a common set of ethical principles." The authors' attention is largely directed toward Gandhi's principles for sociopolitical action. The article was written after a seminar on Gandhi at the Institute for Social Research, Oslo.

Jaspers, Karl. *Die Atombombe und die Zukunft des Menschen,* München: R. Piper & Co. Verlag, 1958. Contains some material on Gandhi's method. English translation, *The Future of Mankind,* Chicago: University of Chicago Press, 1961.

King, Martin Luther, Jr. *Stride Toward Freedom. The Montgomery Story,* with a foreword by Trevor Huddleston, C. R., London: Gollancz, 1959. Account of and commentary on the Negro bus boycott in Montgomery, Alabama, and on the significance of nonviolent opposition in the struggle against racial discrimination. King's contribution is in the Gandhian spirit.

King-Hall, Commander Sir Stephen. *Defence in the Nuclear Age,* London: Gollancz, 1957. A military-grounded plea for unilateral nuclear disarmament and the introduction of nonviolent opposition as a political measure. Strongly influenced by Gandhian pacifism.

Lewis, John. *The Case Against Pacifism,* London: Allen and Unwin, 1937. One of the few systematic attempts at a critical examination of the weaknesses in the arguments for pacifism.

Little, Bradford. *National Defense Through Nonviolent Resistance,* Chicago: own publisher, 1958. The author accepts the necessity of defense against foreign aggression and sketches what steps should be taken should the United States replace its military defense system with a nonviolent one.

Mills, C. Wright. *The Causes of World War Three,* London: Secker and Warburg, 1959. A stimulating book by an American sociologist about the bases of the increasing tendency toward war.

Morris-Jones, W. H. "Mahatma Gandhi—Political Thinker?" *Political Studies,* Vol. 8, 1960, pp. 16-36. Morris-Jones is a professor of political theory and political institutions. His careful conclusions are of great interest for the clarification of how representatives of a central academic discipline view Gandhi's contribution.

Narayan, Jayaprakash. *From Socialism to Sarvodaya,* Kashi: Akhil Bharat Sarva Seva Sangh Prakashan, Rajghat, 1958. The author's ideological shift from socialism to nonviolent social revolution in India. Narayan was leader of the socialist party and was expected to become Nehru's successor.

Naess, Arne. "Systematization of Gandhian Ethics of Conflict Resolution." *Journal of Conflict Resolution,* Vol. II, no. 2 (June 1958), pp. 140-55. A systematic reconstruction of that part of Gandhi's system which relates to political conflict, and a discussion of the significance of Gandhi's contribution to international cooperation and to social science research.

Non-violence in Peace and War, extracts from *Harijan* made by M. Derai, Vol. I, Ahmedabad: Navajivan, 1942, 489 pp. Also accounts of conversations, all from the years 1920-42. Detailed register; very valuable source book.

Non-violence in Peace and War, Vol. 2, continuation of the above. Extracts from *Harijan* and conversations in the years 1946 to Gandhi's death. Published by B. Kumarappa. Ahmedabad: Navajivan, 1949, 394 pp.

Prabhu, R. K. and U. R. Rao (compilers). *The Mind of Mahatma Gandhi,* with a foreword by Sir Sarvepalli Radhakrishnan, Bombay: Oxford University Press, 1945. A short but excellent collection of brief quotations of Gandhi on a range of religious, social and political questions.

Pyarelal. *Mahatma Gandhi. The Last Phase,* Ahmedabad: Navajivan Publishing House, Vol. I, 1956, Vol. II, 1958. A thorough study of Gandhi's last four years. See especially Vol. II, pp. 484-510, on Kashmir.

Rao, G. Ramachandra. *An Atheist with Gandhi,* Ahmedabad: Navajivan Publishing House, (1951) 1958. An atheistic social worker's account of his correspondence and conversations with Gandhi on the subject of atheism.

Sharma, B. S. *The Political Philosophy of Mahatma Gandhi in relation to the English Liberal Tradition.* Doctoral thesis (London 1955), in which the author, among other things, stresses the important points of resemblance between Th. H. Green and Gandhi. This thesis was later included in the same author's *Gandhi as a Political Thinker,* Allahabad, 1957.

Sharp, Gene. "The Constructive Programme," *Mankind,* Vol. I, no. 12 (July 1957), pp. 1102-12. The constructive program for the construction of a nonviolent social order.

Sharp, Gene. *Gandhi Wields the Weapon of Moral Power. Three Case Histories,* with a foreword by Albert Einstein. Ahmedabad: Navajivan Publishing House, 1960.

Sharp, Gene. "The Meanings of Non-violence, A Typology (Revised)," *Journal of Conflict Resolution,* Vol. III, no. 1 (March 1959), pp. 41-66. A classification of nine types of absence of physical violence, with references to the literature of the topic.

Sharp, Gene (in collaboration with Johan Galtung). "Unarmed Strategy. Notes on Research and Analysis of Non-violent Struggles," *Mankind,* Vol. III, no. 1 (August 1958). Detailed plan for the analysis of nonviolent struggle with reference to the increase of its future effectiveness.

Spitz, David. "Democracy and the Problem of Civil Disobedience," *The American Political Science Review,* Vol. 48, no. 2 (June 1954), pp. 386-403. Analysis of the question of whether civil disobedience is justified in a political democracy.

Wolff, Otto. *Mahatma und Christus, Eine Charakter-studie Mahatma Gandhis and des Modernen Hinduismus,* Berlin: Lettner-Verlag, 1955. An influential negative evaluation of Gandhi, based on recent orthodox Protestant theology, and anti-Gandhi stories.

Young India, weekly newspaper, published in Ahmedabad, edited by Gandhi from October 1919 until February 1932.